CU00793078

WHISKY
in Your
POCKET

To the memory of Duncan McGillivray of Bruichladdich
1952–2020
Once met, never forgotten

WHISKY
in Your
POCKET

NEIL WILSON

WAVERLEY BOOKS

Published in 2021 by Waverley Books, an imprint of
The Gresham Publishing Company Ltd,
31, Six Harmony Row, Glasgow, G51 3BA, Scotland

www.waverley-books.co.uk
info@waverley-books.co.uk
facebook/pages/waverleybooks

First published 2010. This fully revised 10th edition published 2021
Printed in China

ISBN 978-1-84934-533-0

Contents

Introduction

THE introduction to the first edition of *Whisky in Your Pocket* was written by Wallace Milroy in 2010. Sadly he passed away late in 2016 and so the onus of taking on all the writing chores for this new edition has fallen to me. To say that Wallace was a giant in the field of Scotch malt whisky is an understatement and his passing was marked by many prominent members of the industry. The growth of the popularity of the single malt sector owes much to the efforts he and his brother Jack made in central London back in the 1960s and 70s.

But time marches on and the challenges of Brexit now stare the Scotch whisky industry straight in the face. As I write the circumstances of the UK's future relationship with the EU is simply unknown so I will not make any predictions as to how, over the course of the remaining months in 2020, this will pan out and I will concentrate on what the reader can gain from studying this volume. Its forerunner was *Wallace Milroy's Malt Whisky Almanac*, first published in 1986, which evolved over seven editions, reaching 350,000 sales with foreign editions also published in Japan, USA, Canada, Germany and Italy. The seventh edition came out in 1998 and after that Wallace and I decided to rest the project for a while as it was competing in an overcrowded marketplace and had served its purpose well in introducing people to the world of malt whisky.

By 2009 we decided to republish the book under a new title through Waverley Books of Glasgow which brought extra marketing and promotional muscle and very high standards of production quality. A decade has now passed and this new edition comes at a time when the Scotch single malt sector has never been so buoyant with the expansion of a number of established distilleries and many new ones, of various capacities, emerging in almost every corner of the country, a phenomenon which is being matched around the world.

Given this rate of expansion a new edition was necessary and I hope that it will remain the 'go to' pocket refer-

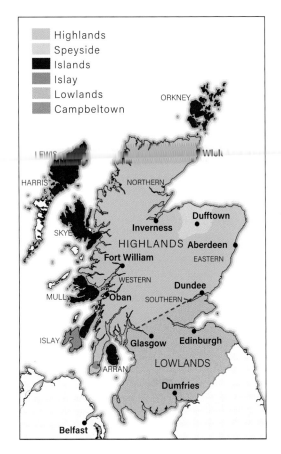

Highlands
Speyside
Islands
Islay
Lowlands
Campbeltown

ORKNEY

LEWIS

Wick

HARRIS

NORTHERN

SKYE

Dufftown

Inverness

HIGHLANDS Aberdeen

EASTERN

Fort William

WESTERN

MULL

Dundee

Oban

SOUTHERN

ISLAY

Glasgow Edinburgh

ARRAN

LOWLANDS

Dumfries

Belfast

ence guide to be carried by anyone with an interest in Scotch whisky, whether an old hand or a newcomer. In that latter role it was always Wallace's intention for the book to quell the nerves of 'confused consumers' making their way down the supermarket spirits' aisle, or venturing through airside shopping areas and being faced with a vast number of differing bottlings. To that end, after the preliminaries, the book remains structured by producing region starting with Speyside, then the geographically vast Highlands which are broken down into Eastern, Northern, Southern and Western, followed by the rapidly expanding Lowlands, then Islay and Campbeltown until we round off with the Islands.

Wallace always felt that the regional classification created by the Scotch Whisky Association (SWA), the official trade organisation body, was in need of revision. The SWA includes the Islands in the Highlands region and it was always a source of amusement to him as to how Highland Park on Orkney and Glengoyne in Stirlingshire were considered to be in the same producing area. Historically only two producing 'regions' used to exist, the Highlands and the Lowlands, separated by an imaginary line, drawn up in the Wash Act of 1784, from Greenock to Dundee, either side of which was subject to differing excise regulations. In the Highlands the small-batch, pot-still process was employed whereas the Lowland distillers used the high-volume, large-batch, flash-distillation technique. With the rise of blending in the mid-to-late 19th century, malt distilleries were ranked by blenders into classes from Top, through First, Second and Third Class and generally speaking all the top-ranked whiskies were Speysides. Thus regional styles were applied and have tended to stick largely because the big distillers needed to manage large amounts of stock for blending in a comprehensible manner.

If there is one overriding factor that has driven the many new expressions to have been created over the last decade, it is flavour. No longer is the industry tied to the geographical, terroir-based, limitations nor to the traditional age-specific releases. Now, management of stocks is all tied to how to drive the flavour of a whisky. There are now so many available no-age-statement (**NAS**) expressions available that it is impossible to cover them all in the compass of this slim volume. For that reason the whiskies detailed herein refer to the main UK trade bottling, whether age-related or not.

The tasting notes used in this book are those of the proprietors where available (or the independent bottler) and describe the whisky after water has been added, unless stated. Any set of notes is subjective, but these are here to help, not to hinder, and have been rendered as simply as possible. The addition of water is to your taste but some malts do not require them and can be treated like a fine cognac or armagnac after dinner. All cask-strength single malts and grains should have some water added (bit by bit ... you can always add water but never take it away!) but you can taste a small amount at full strength first. All the notes refer to 70cl bottle volume unless otherwise stated and the acronym **STR** refers to casks that have been 'shaved, toasted and re-charred'.

As alluded to earlier, a large number of new distilling operations have sprung up since the start of the millennium and one very small operator, the Loch Ewe Distillery at Aultbea has closed. (Another to disappear was the short-lived Deeside Distillery at Banchory which undertook a short season of distilling in order to create 100 casks, 88 of which were for private customers. The proceeds are hoped to underwrite a larger distilling operation nearby.) Many of the ongoing works are still at the planning stages or are continuing a very lengthy gestation period such as Falkirk Distillery, but others are now operational after relatively short periods. As I write a distillery in my home town of Moffat, Dumfriesshire, has had its planning application granted and construction should start soon. I have tried to include all of the newer distilleries that have actually laid down whisky stocks or have plans to do so, although tasting samples may not have been available. Companies that are distilling or rectifying purely for the production of gin, with no plans for whisky production, are excluded. Similarly rum distillation is not included although I believe this will be a growth category for distillation in Scotland. Another notable development has been the announcement from Diageo to reinstate distilling at Port Ellen Distillery on Islay and Brora in Sutherland. Similarly Rosebank at Camelon, Falkirk is set to start production soon under the new owners, Ian Macleod Distillers.

The industry can be described as still being driven globally by blended Scotch sales, with a healthy but still relatively small single-malt category and a growing artisanal craft-distilling sector which is showing the most innovation in terms of how whiskies are distilled and matured. In June 2019 the SWA altered the regulations which determine the type of wood in which Scotch whisky can be matured including those previously used to age agave spirits (including Tequila and mezcal), Calvados, barrel-aged cachaça, shochu and baijiu, as well as some other fruit spirits. The possible effects of these changes are some way off, but should increase the appeal of Scotch whisky to a wider market.

New-make spirit is now something that is no longer considered solely for onward maturation to legal whisky status at three years, but can be found being sold commercially such as Lindores Abbey Aqua Vitae and Annandale's Rascally Liquor. These young, characterful spirits are increasingly popular with mixologists as the base alcohol in new cocktails.

The other educational issue which was introduced in the last edition is the question of what actually constitutes 'Scotch whisky'. This book clearly defines the five types of Scotch that currently make up the sector: single malt, blended malt, single grain, blended grain and blended Scotch. Chapter 1 deals with this in greater depth and it is not as confusing as it sounds once the production processes for single malt and single grain are understood, as described in Chapter 2.

Diageo remains the giant in the industry with 28 malt distilleries, followed by Pernod-Ricard, operated by Chivas Brothers (13). The other main operators in alphabetic order are Angus Dundee Distillers (2), Beam Suntory (5), BenRiach Distillery Co, owned by Brown-Forman (3), Burn Stewart Distillers Ltd, owned by Distell Group Ltd (3), Edrington (3), Inver House Distillers Ltd, owned by ThaiBev (5), John Dewar & Sons Ltd, owned by Bacardi Ltd (5), Whyte & Mackay Ltd, owned by Emperador (4), William Grant & Sons Ltd (4), Loch Lomond Group, owned by Hillhouse Capital Management (2), Glenmorangie PLC, owned by LVMH (2), Isle of Arran Distillers Ltd (2), Ian Macleod Distillers Ltd (2), Campari Group (1), Signatory Vintage Scotch Whisky Co Ltd (1), Takara Shuzo Co Ltd (1), J&G Grant (1), Rémy Cointreau (1), Gordon & MacPhail (1), Ben Nevis Distillery (Fort William) Ltd, owned by Asahi Group Holdings (1) and La Martiniquaise (1). A further 34 companies are operators of an active single malt whisky distillery, taking the current total to 125.

The grain whisky sector is represented with seven distilleries controlled by Diageo (Cameronbridge), William Grant & Sons Ltd (Girvan), Lothian Distillers Ltd trading as North British Distillery Co Ltd (Edinburgh), Whyte & Mackay Ltd (Invergordon), Loch Lomond Group (Loch Lomond), La Martiniquaise (Starlaw) and Chivas Brothers (Strathclyde).

It is from this range of malt and grain distilleries that the entire output of Scotch whisky is distilled and then sold on at home and abroad, in bottled and bulk form, contributing some £4.7 billion to the UK exchequer.

Enjoy your journey with *Whisky in Your Pocket*!

Neil Wilson, December 2020.

1. What is Scotch Whisky?

WHEN you buy Scotch whisky it will come in a bottle. You can buy it in bulk in a cask, but very few people have the means to do this. There are **five** types of Scotch whisky which were redefined in November 2009, exactly 100 years after a Royal Commission had defined what Scotch whisky was following a scandal involving the adulteration of whisky being sold in pubs. At that time whisky was distilled in two ways: in batches using pot stills and in a continuous method using the large, industrial patent still. Prior to the 1909 ruling, the Highland pot-still malt whisky distillers considered their whisky to be the true Scotch while the larger patent-still grain distillers were accused of passing off their less reputable whisky as the real thing. The commission settled the matter by stating that Scotch whisky was spirit distilled in Scotland from a mash of cereals which had been converted into soluble sugars by the action of the enzyme diastase contained within the malted portion of the mash. Effectively that meant that the produce of both distillation techniques was Scotch whisky.[1] The finding was a victory for the Lowland patent-still producers and from that point onwards the industry evolved into what it is today: a worldwide, multi-million dollar success story.

The bottle you buy will therefore contain one or other of these two types of whisky or a mixture of them. Under the definitions the most common of the five forms of bottled whisky is **blended Scotch**.

The graphic shows a typical bottle of this type of Scotch, made up of 40% malt whisky and 60% grain whisky but these proportions will vary from producer to producer. One popular blended Scotch, Teacher's Highland Cream, has a 45% malt whisky proportion. More commonly, the malt proportion is likely to be around 25%. The portion of malt can consist of

---

[1] After the 1909 ruling some changes were made in 1915 requiring whisky to be matured in casks for at least three years. The strength at which whisky can be distilled must be no more than 94.8% alcohol.

as many individual malt whiskies as the blender decides to use, while the grain portion can also consist of more than one grain whisky, but as there are only seven grain distilleries in Scotland blenders tend to choose from a much reduced

BLENDED SCOTCH

VARIABLE PROPORTION OF GRAIN

AND MALT WHISKIES

palette. Anyone shopping in a supermarket will see perhaps a dozen blended Scotch whiskies for sale including Johnnie Walker, Teacher's, Bell's, Whyte & Mackay, High Commissioner and The Famous Grouse. None of these brands carry an age statement on the label, but many of them issue aged expressions which are more expensive. The **minimum legal strength** for all five types of bottled Scotch is **40% abv** (alcohol by volume) and any age statement on the label will refer to the **youngest** whisky in the bottling, irrespective of whether it is within the malt portion or the grain portion.

The next category our supermarket shopper is likely to find is **single malt Scotch**. This whisky is produced in batches using the pot-still distilling process employed at all of Scotland's 125 active malt distilleries. Malt whisky is made from 100% malted barley, unlike grain whisky which is made from

SINGLE MALT

100% MALT WHISKY FROM ONE DISTILLERY

LAPHROAIG

ISLAY SINGLE MALT SCOTCH WHISKY

AGED **10** YEARS

EST 1815

a mixture of cereals. Brands include Glenfiddich, Laphroaig, Macallan, Dalmore, Talisker, Highland Park, Jura, Bladnoch, Springbank and The Deveron amongst many others.

The contents of the bottle you purchase will contain pure malt whisky from the distillery named on the label which may, or may not, carry an age statement. If it does then the age of the youngest malt within the bottle will be the age stated on the label. This is sometimes a confusing issue for the consumer but it shows that in order to produce a consistent product distillers will marry aged vintages of malt from the same distillery. So a bottle of single malt may contain malts distilled at different times from the same distillery. Rarer malts from single casks will carry an age statement and sometimes the number of the cask or bottle and the year of distillation. These will also be bottled at a higher strength than usual as these whiskies are not diluted down to the minimum legal strength of 40% abv.

The remaining categories represent altogether rarer types of Scotch whisky. **Blended malt Scotch** is a blend of two or more single malt Scotch whiskies from different distilleries.[2] Brands that fall into this category include Big Peat, Monkey Shoulder, Johnnie Walker Green Label and Spice Tree.

---

[2] Previously this was referred to as vatted malt Scotch whisky.

Blended grain Scotch is a blend of two or more single grain Scotch whiskies from different distilleries employing the patent-still distillation process. The Snow Grouse was the only readily available brand but has been discontinued. The rarer and more expensive Hedonism from Compass Box is available from specialist retailers and other independent bottlers have also ventured into this category, such as North Star Spirits.

Single grain Scotch is whisky from one grain distillery only. Cameron Brig is the most prominent trade bottling but is only available in Fife and from specialist retailers. Bottlings from defunct grain distilleries are available from independent bottlers and are generally very rare and very expensive.

Now that we know what Scotch whisky is, we can look at how it is made.

2. How is Scotch Whisky Made?

WE know that Scotch whisky exists in two forms; **malt** and **grain**. Now we need to look at how both are produced. Up to the point of **distillation**, the processes are very similar in that a low-alcohol beer is produced, called **wash**. Malt whisky wash is made from only malted barley, whereas grain whisky wash consists of some malted barley, but is predominately wheat-based with maize.

In both cases the cereals used contain energy-rich starch which will be used to produce alcohol, but first it must be converted into soluble sugars. For malt whisky, the barley is **malted** by steeping in water for a couple of days, after which it is allowed to **germinate** over four days. This can be done on traditional **floor maltings** which used to exist in all distilleries but which are now confined to a few including Laphroaig, BenRiach, Bowmore and Balvenie where a proportion of the total malt requirement is made this way.[3]

MAKING MALT WHISKY

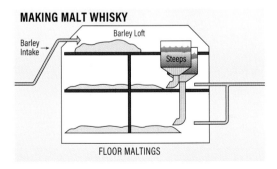

Barley Intake

Barley Loft

Steeps

FLOOR MALTINGS

---

[3] Only Springbank in Campbeltown produces its entire malt requirement on its floor maltings as well as that of its sister distillery, Glengyle.

The modern-day equivalents to floor maltings include the industrial drum maltings which operate in a number of locations around Scotland such as Glen Ord, Burghead and Port Ellen. Other ways to create malt are the Saladin Box process (as once seen at Tamdhu Distillery), the Wanderhaufen system and Tower Maltings, but these last two are more prevalent on the continent. The processes of all these types of maltings might differ, but the result is the same.

Once the starch content has been converted it must be dried to stop further germination and maximize the sugar content. Distilleries that operate floor maltings do this on site by drying the barley in **kilns** topped by distinctive cupola roofs. Depending on the flavour profile of the whisky, peat is used in varying quantities to aid this process and impart 'peatiness' to the malt which is measured as the **phenolic content** in **parts per million** (**ppm**). Many malt distilleries use unpeated malt while others like Laphroaig, Ardmore and Kilchoman, use peated malt at varying phenolic levels. Commercial maltings produce malt to the precise specifications of each individual distillery in large, efficient kilns employing the latest heat-reclamation and drying techniques. Kilning usually takes a couple of days. The grain distillers also use a proportion of this malt in the cereal mash they use as the enzyme, diastase, which is contained within the malt, and diatase is key in breaking down the starch content of the wheat and maize.

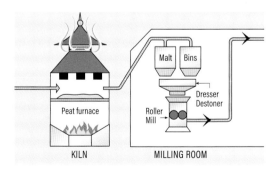

Once the malt is ready it will be crisp, toasted and friable and is ready for **milling**. This is done by passing the mash through a dresser/destoner to remove undesirables before it is ground in a roller mill to a floury grist. In this state it is ready for **mashing**. In the mash house, it is piped into the **mashtun** with hot water and stirred to create a sweet, sugary liquor called **wort**. In the grain whisky process the ground wheat and maize portion of the mash is placed in a pressure cooker and made into a porridge which is then added to the mashtun. Once conversion is complete the mashtun is drained and the wort is processed via a vessel named the **underback** to the wort **cooler** and then transferred to the fermentation vessels in the **tun room**, known as **washbacks**, where **yeast** is added. The residue from the mashtun is processed into animal feed.

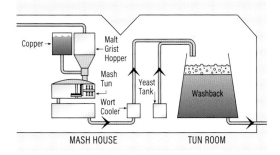

MASH HOUSE   TUN ROOM

Fermentation usually lasts between two to five days and creates a low-alcohol beer with a strength of 7–8% abv and a lot of carbon dioxide which is lost to the atmosphere in most malt distilleries, but is of such significant volume in the grain whisky process that it is captured and processed. Once the wash is ready to be distilled the processes involved in creating malt and grain whisky diverge, so we will deal with malt whisky distillation first.

Malt whisky distilling

IN the **still house**, all malt whisky distilleries employ at least one pair of **pot** stills and sometimes an odd number of them. These are generally onion-shaped at the bottom with a rising, tapering neck section that then turns into a long pipe that carries the distillate away. The stills are generally heated with internal coils charged with steam; the rare exception being direct-fired stills with a gas burner beneath them. The principle of this technique is to distil the low-alcohol wash in the first still (the **wash still**) and to process that distillate (now around 21–23% abv) in the second still (the **low wines** or **spirit still**) to redistill it into spirit between 67–72% abv. The distillate condenses by passing through the coil of copper pipe immersed in cold water in a **worm tub**, or more commonly, through a modern water-cooled **jacket condenser**.

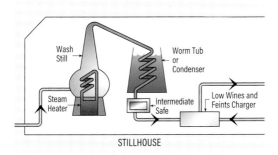

STILLHOUSE

Distillate from the wash still is captured in the **low wines and feints charger** before being used in the second distillation. The run of spirit from the spirit still is monitored and diverted back to the low wines and feints charger until the correct **strength** is obtained when it is diverted into the **spirit receiver**.

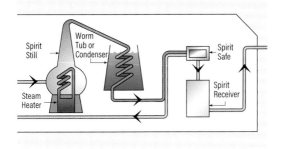

The first part of the distillate that is discarded is called the **foreshots**, the important portion that is captured next is the **middle cut** and the last part, when the alcoholic volume starts to tail off, is called the **feints** which are again diverted to the low wines charger and redistilled in the next batch. The **stillman** makes the decision as to which part of the **spirit run** to collect by checking its strength as it flows through the **spirit safe**.[4] The middle cut is diverted into the spirit receiver tank before being piped to the **spirit store**.

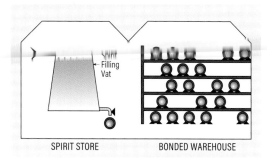

Spirit
← Filling
Vat

SPIRIT STORE   BONDED WAREHOUSE

The residue in the wash still is known as 'pot ale' and is processed into cattle food and usually mixed with the draff from the mashtun to form cattle cake. This process usually takes place at a 'dark grains' plant offsite, but some larger distilleries have their own facilities onsite to undertake this. The other by-product of the distillation process is the residue left in the spirit still which is known as the 'spent lees' and has to be discarded.

Some oddities have occurred in pot-still distilling practices, the Lomond Still probably being the most well-known. These were pot stills with stubby, steam-heated column heads giving a thicker, heavier spirit and were first developed at Hiram Walker's Dumbarton complex in the 1950s. They have been used at Inverleven, Glenburgie (to create Glencraig malt), Miltonduff (Mosstowie) and Scapa where a variant of the still is the last one still in use in Scotland. The Inverleven still has ended up at Bruichladdich where it is used to make The Botanist gin.

---

[4] Another 'intermediate safe' is employed to monitor the strength of the low wines before entering the low wines and feints charger from the wash still.

Grain whisky distilling

ALTHOUGH only carried out at seven locations in Scotland, this process produces by far and away the largest proportion of Scotch whisky distilled each year in Scotland. The distilling

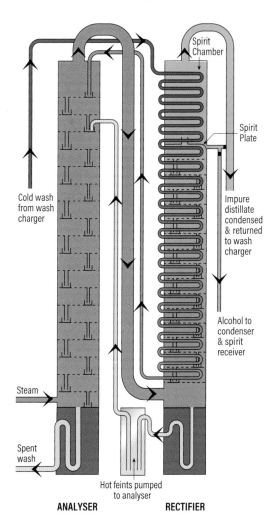

Spirit Chamber

Spirit Plate

Cold wash from wash charger

Impure distillate condensed & returned to wash charger

Alcohol to condenser & spirit receiver

Steam

Spent wash

Hot feints pumped to analyser

ANALYSER   RECTIFIER

process employed at these huge distilleries is a **continuous** process which operates over a period of weeks and months, rather than hours and days. It was invented by Robert Stein of Kilbagie, Clackmannanshire in 1826 and then further developed and refined in 1831 by Aeneas Coffey, whose name is most closely related to the technique.

In its traditional form the still consists of two, tall, interlinked copper and stainless-steel columns, the **analyser** and the **rectifier**, which sit side-by-side. The basic principle is that pressure-fed steam enters the analyser at the base and rises up through a series of compartments separated by perforated sieve plates. As it does so, hot wash is fed in at the top of the analyser and descends through the compartments. The steam strips the alcohol from the wash and carries it over into the base of the rectifier, where it again ascends through another series of compartments. As it does so it comes into contact with the cold wash supply pipe which is routed through the rectifier in a series of loops and coils.[5] This acts as a surface on which the alcohol vapour condenses and the strength of the condensate increases as it rises up the rectifier until it is gathered on top of the unperforated **spirit plate** in the topmost compartment, the **spirit chamber**. The spirit this process produces is relatively flavourless compared to malt spirit, but is of a very high purity at around 94% abv.

Any uncondensed vapour is redistilled via the **wash charger** as is the fluid known as the **hot feints** which are piped away from the bottom of the rectifier and pumped back into the upper section of the analyser and redistilled. Once the spirit has been collected the process returns to the same one as employed in the rest of Scotland's distilleries, the only differences being those of scale and location as some malt distilleries tanker their spirit offsite to facilities that are more suitable for cask-filling, maturing and warehousing.

In the **spirit store** the spirit is piped into the **spirit filling vat** where it is diluted down to the distiller's required strength (usually around 63.5% abv) before being measured into individual **casks**. A record of this procedure is carefully logged for HMRC reports to the government. After this the spirit is subject to the producer's needs in terms of which wood it is matured in, how large the casks are, where it is held for

---

[5] Nowadays the wash is fed pre-heated into the analyser and a cold-water pipe acts as the condensing surface in the rectifier. Vacuum-distilling techniques are also more common in the modern-day patent still.

maturing and for how long. The minimum term is **three years**, after which it can be used for bottling and blending. Almost all of the grain whisky produced in Scotland is released to be used in blending while the malt whisky stocks are carefully monitored and managed to meet the requirements of the master blenders, many of whom have to source malts from other producers to create the blends in their own portfolios. This is when the value of **wood management** becomes most apparent.

When spirit is first placed in a cask it is raw. From that point onwards the wood has an effect on it as the spirit interacts with the soluble constituents of the cask as it breathes, allowing the release of some alcoholic content which weakens the remaining spirit volume.[6] Whisky is always matured in oak of either American or European extraction with most European oak being Spanish in origin. The new regulations of June 2019 also allow maturation in casks previously used to mature agave spirits (including Tequila and mezcal), Calvados, barrel-aged cachaça, shochu and baijiu, as well as some other fruit spirits.

Casks that have previously held bourbon or sherry are common and must be no more than 700 litres in volume and of oak. Casks can be used more than once and can be rejuvenated by replacing old staves and also by using the STR practice.

Many distillers and independent bottlers are now giving maturation details on the bottle labels and packaging so you might see that a malt whisky has been matured for 10 years in ex-bourbon and then finished for 18 months in Oloroso ex-sherry. Blended whiskies tend not to carry any maturation details, but that is changing.

---

[6] This loss is referred to as the 'angels' share' and amounts to 1–2% per annum of all maturing stocks in Scotland.

3. Single Malt Scotch Speyside

THE malts produced in this area of Scotland are perhaps the most obvious answer to the beginner's question, 'What does malt whisky taste like?' and it is more likely that anyone encountering malt for the first time will probably be trying a Glenfiddich or a Glenlivet. But that should not detract from the fact that malt whiskies are distilled over the length and breadth of Scotland and display a remarkable degree of variation.

This area contains the largest concentration of whisky-making apparatus in the world. In total there are 53 distilleries here of which 49 are active. The dormant four are Dallas Dhu (with ongoing plans to reinstate it if its owner, Historic Environment Scotland, can find a funding partner), Coleburn, Convalmore and Parkmore, all three of which will never produce again. There are three which no longer exist: Caperdonich, Imperial and Pittyvaich. The site of Imperial was redeveloped with the establishment of Dalmunach in 2014. Roseisle Distillery, the fourth-largest in Scotland, is not detailed in this section as it has been exclusively distilling for blending purposes since its inception in 2009. There is a planned venture in the area at Cabrach, historically a place of much illicit distillation, but it is not up and running yet and will be a small operation.

Speyside's illicit distilling of the 18th and early 19th centuries gained it a high reputation and it was not until 1823 that the government finally grasped the nettle and introduced legislation that encouraged illicit distillers to take out licences. George Smith of Glenlivet was granted the first of these. He later moved the distillery to its current location at Minmore in 1858 where he conducted business with his son, John. Stylistically the malts from this area are medium- to full-bodied, with some sweetness and they mature well be-

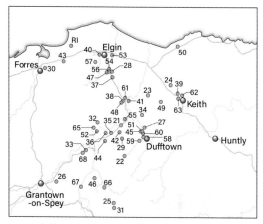

Distillery number refers to page number. RI = Roseisle

tween 10 to 15 years. Some producers age them even more but the bulk of them will be found in this age range or with no age statement. Many are matured in ex-sherry casks and this gives them a rich, savoury finish, which is one of the hallmarks of a Speyside.

This area is one of the most beautiful in Scotland and there are good facilities at many of the distilleries for visitors. There is an established Malt Whisky Trail (http://maltwhiskytrail.com) which consists of Benromach, Cardhu, Glenfiddich, Glen Grant, Glen Moray, Glenlivet, Strathisla and Dallas Dhu along with the Speyside Cooperage in Dufftown. Speyside also hosts two whisky festivals, one in the spring and one in autumn, both ideal times to be in the area (www.spiritofspeyside.com).

From a blending point of view, the Speysides form the backbone of most of the Scotch whisky blends that you will find. So why are they so important to the blender? Richard Paterson, master blender at Whyte & Mackay, draws an interesting comparison between the father of blending, Andrew Usher (1826-98) and Paul Cézanne, the father of modern art. The analogy is a good one in that the master blender 'draws from a palette of malt and grain whiskies to create his masterpieces. Harmony is his ultimate aim. No one colour, no one malt, must predominate.' This palette consists of a large number of malt whiskies and a relatively small number of grain whiskies. The Speysides form the largest part of the malt palette as the heavier and more smoky Islays are used sparingly due to their high degree of influence on the finished product. Other robust malts from the Highlands, Islands and Campbeltown make distinct contributions to the blender's craft depending on their individual character. The floral, aromatic Lowlands help to create balance between these malts and integrate them with the larger grain whisky proportion.

In a word, Speyside is the heart of malt whisky distilling in Scotland and the malts we are now going to look at are the core bottlings which represent distillery character best. Most distilleries issue many more expressions and these can be discovered via the relevant Internet websites for each producer.

Whiskies from lost distilleries such as Coleburn, Dallas Dhu and Pittyvaich have been available occasionally from Diageo's Rare Malts selection, in the Special Releases 'Rare by Nature' and the discontinued (but still available) Flora & Fauna series, or from the numerous specialist retailers and independent bottlers.

Malt	**Aberlour**
Pronounced	*aber-LOWERR*
Distillery	Aberlour
	ABERLOUR
	AB38 9PJ
Owner	Pernod Ricard
Visitors	Tel: 01340 881249
Website	www.aberlour.com
Established	1879
Status	In production
Water source	Birkenbush and other springs
Malt source	Commercial maltsters
Phenols	Unpeated
Casks	Ex-bourbon and ex-sherry
Capacity	3.8 million litres of alcohol
Stills	Wash: 2 Spirit: 2
Main bottling	12 years old, 40%
Nose	Trace of cinnamon with preserved fruit.
Taste	Buttery, syrupy with raisins and a trace of charred wood.
Finish	Medium, fruity, warming.
Comments	A popular, award-winning malt from Speyside.
Also try	Benrinnes, Benromach, Glenturret
Availability	Everywhere
Price	£40

Malt	Allt-a-Bhainne
Pronounced	*olt-a-VAN-ya*
Distillery	Allt-a-Bhainne
	Glenrinnes
	DUFFTOWN
	AB55 4DE
Owner	Pernod Ricard
Established	1975
Status	In production
Water source	Springs on Benrinnes
Malt source	Commercial maltsters
Phenols	Unpeated and medium-peated
Casks	Refill hogsheads
Capacity	4.2 million litres of alcohol
Stills	Wash: 2 Spirit: 2
Main bottling	Distillery Reserve Collection, NAS, 40%
Nose	Smoky hints of peat, some leather and oak.
Taste	Roast fruits and honey hints, with cinnamon spice and peat.
Finish	Long, smooth, gently smoky.
Comments	The first official owner bottling.
Also try	Ardmore, Highland Park, Bowmore
Availability	Specialist retailers
Price	£33

Malt	**Auchroisk**
Pronounced	*ar-thrusk*
Distillery	Auchroisk
	MULBEN
	AB55 6XS
Owner	Diageo
Website	www.malts.com
Established	1974
Status	In production
Water source	Dorie's Well
Malt source	Burghead Maltings
Phenols	Unpeated
Casks	Mostly ex-sherry
Capacity	5.9 million litres of alcohol
Stills	Wash: 4 Spirit: 4
Sample	Flora & Fauna, 10 years old, 43%
Nose	Toffee and malt. Sweet pastry and a light fruitiness like tarte tatin.
Taste	Sweet malt with some acidity. Shortbread and spice. Trace of warm wood in development.
Finish	Warming and long.
Comments	One of Diageo's rare distillery bottlings.
Also try	Glen Keith, Glenrothes, Tormore
Availability	Specialist retailers
Price	£50 plus

Malt	**Aultmore**
Pronounced	*ollt-MORE*
Distillery	Aultmore
	KEITH
	AB55 6QY
Owner	John Dewar & Sons Ltd
Website	www.Aultmore.com
Established	1897
Status	In production
Water source	Auchinderran Dam
Malt source	Commercial maltsters
Phenols	Unpeated
Casks	Ex-bourbon
Capacity	3.2 million litres of alcohol
Stills	Wash: 2 Spirit: 2
Main bottling	12 years old, 46%
Nose	Sweet pear, vanilla and cut grass.
Taste	Fruity with a hint of caramel and spice.
Finish	Refreshing with a hint of spice.
Comments	One of Bacardi's unsung malts.
Also try	Glenmorangie, Knockando, Arran
Availability	Specialist retailers
Price	£45 plus

Malt	**Ballindalloch**
Pronounced	*baal-in-daal-och*
Distillery	Ballindalloch
	Lagmore
	BALLINDALLOCH
	AB37 9AA
Owner	Ballindalloch Distillery LLP
Visitors	By appointment, tel: 01807 500331
Website	www.ballindallochdistillery.com
Established	2014
Status	In production
Water source	Garline Springs
Malt source	Own-estate malted by Bairds
Phenols	Unpeated
Casks	First and refill ex-bourbon with some ex-sherry casks
Capacity	100,000 litres of alcohol
Stills	Wash: 1 Spirit: 1
Sample	New make, 68–69%
Nose	Crisp, clean and fruity derived from long fermentations and slow distilling.
Taste	Sweet and light with notes of tropical fruit. Great balance and a rich, soft mouthfeel.
Finish	Remarkably smooth. Gently lingers with the sweetness remaining.
Comments	A welcome addition to the Speyside stable, but not ready yet. The likely release date will be 2023.
Availability	None at present

Malt	Balmenach
Pronounced	*baal-MENN-ach*
Distillery	Balmenach
	GRANTOWN-ON-SPEY
	PH26 3PF
Owner	Inver House Distillers Ltd
Visitors	By appointment
Website	www.inverhouse.com
Established	c.1824
Status	In production
Water source	Cromdale Burn
Malt source	Commercial maltsters
Phenols	Unpeated
Casks Refill	American and Spanish oak
Capacity	2.8 million litres of alcohol
Stills	Wash: 3 Spirit: 3 Gin: 1
Sample	Master of Malt, 15 years old, 59%
Nose	Fruity, stone fruit mainly, with vanilla and a slaty seaweed-like note.
Taste	Light, fruity, pears and apples, Demerara sugar, then spicy liquorice.
Finish	Fruity, refreshing with a liquorice kick.
Comments	The only malt in the Inver House stable which is not marketed as a brand.
Also try	Glen Grant, Glen Spey, Strathisla
Availability	Specialist retailers, independent bottlers
Price	£36 plus

Malt	**Balvenie**
Pronounced	*baal-VENN-ee*
Distillery	Balvenie DUFFTOWN AB55 4DH
Owner	William Grant & Sons Ltd
Visitors	Tel: 01340 822210
Website	www.thebalvenie.com
Established	1892
Status	In production
Water source	Robbie Dubh Springs
Malt source	Floor maltings, 15% local barley and commercial maltsters
Phenols	Unpeated
Casks	Ex-bourbon and ex-sherry with some port pipes
Capacity	7 million litres of alcohol
Stills	Wash: 5 Spirit: 6
Main bottling	Doublewood, 12 years old, 43%
Nose	Sweet fruit and Oloroso sherry notes, layered with honey and vanilla.
Taste	Smooth and mellow, nutty sweetness, cinnamon spiciness and a delicately proportioned layer of sherry.
Finish	Long and warming.
Comments	Glenfiddich's sister distillery.
Also try	BenRiach, Glendullan, Glenlivet
Availability	Everywhere
Price	£35 plus

Malt	BenRiach
Pronounced	*ben-REE-ach*
Distillery	BenRiach
	ELGIN
	IV30 8SJ
Owner	BenRiach Distillery Co Ltd
Visitors	By appointment, tel: 01343 862888
Website	www.benriachdistillery.com
Established	1898
Status	In production
Water source	Burnside springs
Malt source	Floor malting and commercial maltsters
Phenols	35 ppm and unpeated
Casks	Ex-bourbon and ex-sherry
Capacity	2.8 million litres of alcohol
Stills	Wash: 2 Spirit: 2
Main bottling	10 years old, 43%
Nose	Orchard fruits, hint of vanilla and citrus with sweet barley note.
Taste	Oak spices, dried apricot and peaches, hint of aniseed, lemon zest.
Finish	Long, crisp barley.
Comments	A distillery that is pushing the boundaries of what constitutes regional style.
Also try	Aberlour, Glen Ord, Royal Brackla
Availability	Everywhere
Price	£36 plus

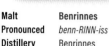

Malt	Benrinnes
Pronounced	*benn-RINN-iss*
Distillery	Benrinnes ABERLOUR AB38 9NN
Owner	Diageo
Website	www.malts.com
Established	c.1826
Status	In production
Water source	Rowantree and Scurran burns
Malt source	Burghead and Roseisle Maltings
Phenols	Unpeated
Casks	Mainly European oak
Capacity	3.5 million litres of alcohol
Stills	Wash: 2 Spirit: 4
Main bottling	Flora & Fauna, 15 years old, 43%
Nose	A rich nose, presenting an early impression of chocolate liqueurs. Light smokiness, and a dense floral note.
Taste	Richly sweet, full, rum-like, with a centre palate impact. In spite of the sweetness, not cloying.
Finish	Dries out slightly, where there is also a 'catch' which might be taken for peat smoke. Medium length, leaving a faintly sherried aftertaste.
Comments	Benrinnes once employed its six stills in a form of triple distillation. Also available bottled as Stronachie.
Also try	Mortlach, Dailuaine, Stronachie
Availability	Specialist retailers, independent bottlers
Price	£36 plus

Malt	**Benromach**
Pronounced	*ben-ROMM-ach*
Distillery	Benromach
	FORRES
	IV36 3EB
Owner	Gordon & MacPhail Ltd
Visitors	By appointment, tel: 01309 675968
Website	www.benromach.com
Established	1898
Status	In production
Water source	Chapelton Springs in the Romach Hills
Malt source	Commercial maltsters
Phenols	Up to 10ppm
Casks	Ex-bourbon and ex-Oloroso sherry
Capacity	700,000 litres of alcohol
Stills	Wash: 1 Spirit: 1 Gin: 1
Main bottling	10 years old, 43%
Nose	Charred oak influence and malt. Slightly nutty with pineapple and kiwi fruit.
Taste	Mouth-coating with toasted malt. Lingering sweet sherry and delicate peat smoke.
Finish	Long and lingering with subtle sherry and peat.
Comments	Rescued in 1993 by Gordon & MacPhail, this is a fine visitor attraction.
Also try	Edradour, Longmorn, Strathisla
Availability	Specialist retailers
Price	£34 plus

Malt	**Braeval**
Pronounced	*bray-VAAL*
Distillery	Braeval
	Chapeltown of Glenlivet
	BALLINDALLOCH
	AB37 9JS
Owner	Pernod Ricard
Established	1973
Status	In production
Water source	Preenie and Katie wells
Malt source	Commercial maltsters
Phenols	Unpeated
Casks	Ex-bourbon
Capacity	4.2 million litres of alcohol
Stills	Wash: 2 Spirit: 4
Sample	Clan Denny, 10 years old, 46%
Nose	Light, dry with honey and fruity notes.
Taste	Medium-bodied, quite sweet with some fruit.
Finish	Refreshing, some spice and a hint of smoke.
Comments	Formerly called Braes of Glenlivet. A whisky largely used for blending.
Also try	Benromach, Auchroisk, Knockando
Availability	Specialist retailers, independent bottlers
Price	£35 plus

Malt	**Cardhu**
Pronounced	*kaar-doo*
Distillery	Cardhu
	Knockando
	ABERLOUR
	AB38 7RZ
Owner	Diageo
Visitors	Tel: 01479 874635. Book tours online
Website	www.malts.com
Established	1824
Status	In production
Water source	Springs on Mannoch Hill and the Lyne Burn
Malt source	Burghead Maltings
Phenols	Unpeated
Casks	Refill ex-bourbon hogsheads
Capacity	3.4 million litres of alcohol
Stills	Wash: 3 Spirit: 3
Sample	12 years old, 40%
Nose	Heady, pear drops, heather, resin and sweet honey-nut notes.
Taste	Medium-bodied. Well balanced, smooth mouthfeel; sweet and fresh then drying.
Finish	Lingering sweet smoke. Attractive, drying aftertaste.
Comments	A signature malt in the Johnnie Walker blends.
Also try	Glen Grant, Speyside, anCnoc
Availability	Everywhere
Price	£35 plus

Malt	Cragganmore
Pronounced	*crag-ann-MORE*
Distillery	Cragganmore
	BALLINDALLOCH
	AB37 9AB
Owner	Diageo
Visitors	Tel: 01479 874715. Book tours online
Website	www.malts.com
Established	1869
Status	In production
Water source	Craggan Burn
Malt source	Roseisle Maltings
Phenols	Lightly peated.
Casks	Ex-bourbon and sherry
Capacity	2.2 million litres of alcohol
Stills	Wash: 2 Spirit: 2
Main bottling	12 years old, 40%
Nose	Sweet floral fragrances, riverside herbs and flowers with some honey and vanilla.
Taste	Strong malty taste. Hints of sweet woodsmoke and sandalwood. Firm, rounded, slight to medium.
Finish	A long, malt-driven finish with light smoke and hints of sweetness.
Comments	A malty and complex dram.
Also try	Aberlour, Glenfarclas, Strathisla
Availability	Widespread
Price	£36 plus

Malt	**Craigellachie**
Pronounced	*craig-ELL-achay*
Distillery	Craigellachie
	ABERLOUR
	AB38 9TF
Owner	John Dewar & Sons Ltd
Website	www.Craigellachie.com
Established	1891
Status	In production
Water source	Bluehill Quarry
Malt source	Commercial maltsters
Phenols	Unpeated
Casks	Ex-bourbon and ex-sherry
Capacity	4.1 million litres of alcohol
Stills	Wash: 2 Spirit: 2
Main bottling	13 years old, 40%
Nose	Orchard fruit with sweet caramel hints.
Taste	Rich, malty flavour emerges from caramelised fruit and summer berries and almonds.
Finish	Long, delicately dry finish with a suggestion of charred oak.
Comments	Another constituent malt for the Dewar's blends.
Also try	Ardmore, Glenmorangie, Tamnavulin.
Availability	Specialist retailers
Price	£45 plus

Malt	Dailuaine
Pronounced	*daal-EWE-ann*
Distillery	Dailuaine
	CARRON
	AB38 7RE
Owner	Diageo
Website	www.malts.com
Established	1851
Status	In production
Water source	Balliemullich Burn
Malt source	Burghead Maltings
Phenols	Unpeated
Casks	Refill ex-bourbon hogsheads with some ex-sherry butts
Capacity	5.2 million litres of alcohol
Stills	Wash: 3 Spirit: 3
Main bottling	Flora & Fauna, 16 years old, 43%
Nose	Full, rich, fruity aroma with honeysuckle overtones.
Taste	Full of Speyside flavour. Fruity, full-bodied, nutty, sweet.
Finish	Rich and dry with a long sweet aftertaste.
Comments	A great after-dinner dram.
Also try	Mortlach, Glenfarclas, GlenDronach
Availability	Specialist retailers, independent bottlers
Price	£46 plus

Malt	Dalmunach
Pronounced	*daal-MOON-ach*
Distillery	Dalmunach
	CARRON
	AB38 7QP
Owner	Pernod Ricard
Established	2015
Status	In production
Water source	Ballintomb Burn and three boreholes
Malt source	Bairds Maltings, Pencaitland or Arbroath Maltings
Phenols	Unpeated
Casks	American oak
Capacity	10 million litres of alcohol
Stills	Wash: 4 Spirit: 4
Sample	Limited release, 4 years old, 64.5%
Nose	Green apples, ripe bananas, vanilla.
Taste	Zesty, lemon curd, hint of cinnamon.
Finish	Delicate and sweet.
Comments	Only 348 bottles available.
Also try	Aberlour, Glenlivet, Longmorn
Availability	Only at Strathisla, Glenlivet, Aberlour and Scapa distilleries
Price	£45

Malt	Glen Elgin
Pronounced	*glen ELL-gin*
Distillery	Glen Elgin
	Longmorn
	ELGIN
	IV30 8SL
Owner	Diageo
Visitors	By appointment, tel: 01343 862100
Website	www.malts.com
Established	1900
Status	In production
Water source	Local springs near Millbuies Loch
Malt source	Burghead Maltings
Phenols	Unpeated
Casks	Ex-bourbon and ex-sherry refills
Capacity	2.7 million litres of alcohol
Stills	Wash: 3 Spirit: 3
Main bottling	12 years old, 43%
Nose	Sweet. Almonds, or maybe marzipan. Some orange juice. Perhaps a trace of sawn wood.
Taste	Sweetish, then dryish, with some acidity between; all well balanced.
Finish	Dryish, balanced finish.
Comments	A top blending malt.
Also try	Old Pulteney, Aberfeldy, Arran
Availability	Specialist retailers
Price	£40 plus

Malt	**Glen Grant**
Distillery	Glen Grant
	Elgin Road
	ROTHES
	AB38 7BS
Owner	Campari
Visitors	Tel: 01340 832118
Website	www.glengrant.com
Established	1840
Status	In production
Water source	Caperdonich Well
Malt source	Commercial maltsters
Phenols	Unpeated
Casks	Refill American oak casks
Capacity	6.2 million litres of alcohol
Stills	Wash: 4 Spirit: 4
Main bottling	10 years old, 40%
Nose	Medium-dry, with a good balance of ripe orchard fruits.
Taste	Creamy and fruity.
Finish	Slightly nutty, intense, fruity.
Comments	An excellent introduction to Speyside.
Also try	Auchroisk, GlenAllachie, Knockando
Availability	Widespread
Price	£30 plus

Malt	Glen Keith
Distillery	Glen Keith
	Station Road
	KEITH
	AB55 5BU
Owner	Pernod Ricard
Established	1957–8
Status	In production
Water source	Balloch Hill Springs
Malt source	Commercial maltsters
Phenols	Unpeated
Casks	American oak
Capacity	6.2 million litres of alcohol
Stills	Wash: 3 Spirit: 3
Main bottling	NAS, 40%
Nose	Orchard fruits with a hint of banana.
Taste	Sweet and fruity with floral notes and some vanilla.
Finish	Zesty and spicy with new oak.
Comments	Re-opened in 2013.
Also try	Glen Elgin, Glen Grant, Glenfiddich
Availability	Specialist retailers
Price	£30 plus

Malt	**Glen Moray**
Distillery	Glen Moray
	ELGIN
	IV30 1YE
Owner	La Martiniquaise
Visitors	Tel: 01343 542577
Website	www.glenmoray.com
Established	1897
Status	In production
Water source	River Lossie
Malt source	Commercial maltsters
Phenols	Unpeated
Casks	First and refill ex-bourbon with some ex-sherry casks
Capacity	5.7 million litres of alcohol
Stills	Wash: 2 Spirit: 2
Main bottling	NAS, 40%
Nose	Fragrant, lightly drying, warming malty notes. Butterscotch, shortbread, fresh herbal/grassy notes.
Taste	Lightly spiced with a warming mouthfeel. Malty toffee sweetness, blackcurrants, fragrant citrus lemongrass tang.
Finish	Shortbread, fresh lemongrass, spicy ginger marmalade.
Comments	An excellent distillery to visit.
Also try	Bladnoch, GlenAllachie, Deanston
Availability	Everywhere
Price	£22 plus

Malt	Glen Spey
Distillery	Glen Spey
	ROTHES
	AB38 7AT
Owner	Diageo
Website	www.malts.com
Established	1878
Status	In production
Water source	Doonie Burn
Malt source	Burghead Maltings
Phenols	Unpeated
Casks	Refill ex-bourbon hogsheads
Capacity	1.4 million litres of alcohol
Stills	Wash: 2 Spirit: 2
Main bottling	Flora & Fauna, 12 years old, 43%
Nose	Mild, closed. Lightly fruity like greengages and white grapes. With water, fresh and estery, but still relatively closed.
Taste	Warming. Light sweetness, some acidity.
Finish	Dry, medium length. Some chocolate and light coconut in the aftertaste.
Comments	Much of the production goes into the J&B blend.
Also try	Glen Keith, Glenfiddich, Speyburn
Availability	Specialist retailers, independent bottlers
Price	£46 plus

Malt	**GlenAllachie**
Pronounced	*glen-ALLA-chay*
Distillery	Glenallachie
	ABERLOUR
	AB38 9LR
Owner	Glenallachie Distillers Co Ltd
Visitors	Tel: 01340 872547
Website	www.theglenallachie.com
Established	1967–8
Status	In production
Water source	Henshead and Blackstank Burns
Malt source	Commercial maltsters
Phenols	Unpeated
Casks	Refill hogsheads, butts and barrels
Capacity	4 million litres of alcohol
Stills	Wash: 2 Spirit: 2
Main bottling	12 years old, 46%
Nose	Dark chocolate, raisins and heather honey, with layers of sweet spice and orange peel.
Taste	Rich notes of dark chocolate, raisins, treacle and heather honey, with sweet spices, orange peel and hints of eucalyptus.
Finish	Full and fragrant.
Comments	One of the three distilleries created by Welshman William Delmé-Evans, now under the ownership of Billy Walker.
Also try	Benromach, BenRiach, GlenDronach
Availability	Specialist retailers
Price	£54 plus

Malt	Glenburgie
Pronounced	*glen-BURR-gay*
Distillery	Glenburgie
	FORRES
	IV36 2QY
Owner	Pernod Ricard
Visitors	By appointment, tel: 01343 850258
Established	1829 as Kilnflat. Renamed 1871
Status	In production
Water source	Springs on Burgie Hill and borehole aquifer
Malt source	Commercial maltsters
Phenols	Unpeated
Casks	Refill hogsheads, butts and barrels
Capacity	4.25 million litres of alcohol
Stills	Wash: 3 Spirit: 3
Main bottling	15 years old, 40%
Nose	Complex with syrup, apples, sweet cereal.
Taste	Caramel, chocolate and white pepper then tropical fruits.
Finish	Pleasant but quite short.
Comments	A refreshing malt for pre-dinner drinking. Distillery is beautifully situated.
Also try	Glen Grant, Caperdonich, Inchgower
Availability	Specialist retailers
Price	£44 plus

Malt	Glenfarclas
Distillery	*Glenfarclas*
	Marypark
	BALLINDALLOCH
	AB37 9BD
Owner	J&G Grant
Visitors	Book tours with VisitorCentre@glenfarclas.com
Website	www.glenfarclas.com
Established	1836
Status	In production
Water source	The Green Burn on Ben Rinnes
Malt source	Commercial maltsters
Phenols	1-3 ppm
Casks	Ex-sherry and plain oak
Capacity	3.5 million litres of alcohol
Stills	Wash: 3 Spirit: 3
Main bottling	10 years old, 40%
Nose	Sherry-sweet malty tones with delicate smokiness, releasing subtle spices. Warming the glass reveals honey, vanilla and pear drops.
Taste	Light, with a mouth-watering combination of malt, smoke and sherry sweetness. Hints of dried fruit, vanilla, cinnamon and cloves.
Finish	Long, smooth and spicy, with a delicious, yet delicate, lingering smokiness.
Comments	A big, classic Speyside malt for after dinner.
Also try	Glenlivet, GlenDronach, Mortlach
Availability	Widespread
Price	£33 plus

Malt	Glenfiddich
Pronounced	*glen-FIDD-ich*
Distillery	Glenfiddich
	DUFFTOWN
	AB55 4DH
Owner	William Grant & Sons Ltd
Visitors	Tel: 01340 820373
Website	www.glenfiddich.com
Established	1886–7
Status	In production
Water source	Robbie Dubh Springs
Malt source	Commercial maltsters
Phenols	Unpeated
Casks	American and European oak
Capacity	13.7 million litres of alcohol
Stills	Wash: 11 Spirit: 20
Main bottling	12 years old, 40%
Nose	Fresh and fruity with a hint of pear. Beautifully crafted single malt with a delicately balanced fragrance.
Taste	Characteristic sweet, fruity notes. Develops into elements of butterscotch, cream, malt and subtle oak flavour.
Finish	Long, smooth and mellow.
Comments	The world's most popular single malt.
Also try	Aberlour, Glenmorangie, Glenlivet
Availability	Everywhere
Price	£30 plus

Malt	**Glenlivet**
Distillery	*Glenlivet*
	BALLINDALLOCH
	AB37 9DB
Owner	Pernod Ricard
Visitors	Tel: 01340 821720
Website	www.theglenlivet.com
Established	1824
Status	In production
Water source	Josie's and Blairfindy's wells
Malt source	Portgordon Maltings
Phenols	Unpeated
Casks	American first fill oak
Capacity	21 million litres of alcohol
Stills	Wash: 14 Spirit: 14
Main bottling	Founder's Reserve, NAS, 40%
Nose	Citrus fruit, sweet orange.
Taste	Zesty orange, pear, toffee apples.
Finish	Lingering and gentle.
Comments	Now Scotland's largest malt whisky distillery.
Also try	Glenfarclas, Mortlach, Glenfiddich
Availability	Everywhere
Price	£34 plus

Malt	Glenlossie
Pronounced	*glen-loss-ee*
Distillery	Glenlossie
	ELGIN
	IV30 8SS
Owner	Diageo
Website	www.malts.com
Established	1876
Status	In production
Water source	Bardon Burn
Malt source	Burghead Maltings
Phenols	Unpeated
Casks	Ex-bourbon casks
Capacity	3.7 million litres of alcohol
Stills	Wash: 3 Spirit: 3
Main bottling	Flora & Fauna, 10 years old, 43%
Nose	Vinous, like a well-used cocktail cabinet. Fresh plums and kiwi-fruit and promise of pear drops.
Taste	Sweet. A good balance of primary tastes with some acidity. Very slight hint of smoke when more water is added.
Finish	Dryish, with hints of chocolate notes and a light, malty aftertaste.
Comments	A great aperitif whisky.
Also try	Glen Grant, Knockando, Glen Moray
Availability	Specialist retailers
Price	£48 plus

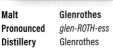

Malt	**Glenrothes**
Pronounced	*glen-ROTH-ess*
Distillery	Glenrothes
	ROTHES
	AB38 7AA
Owner	Edrington Group
Website	www.glenrotheswhisky.com
Established	1878
Status	In production
Water source	Ardcanny and Brauchhill Spring
Malt source	Commercial maltsters
Phenols	Unpeated
Casks	Refill ex-sherry Spanish and American oak and a small proportion of ex-bourbon
Capacity	5.6 million litres of alcohol
Stills	Wash: 5 Spirit: 5
Main bottling	10 years old, 40%
Nose	Toffee and caramel.
Taste	Biscuity and butterscotch, some lemon zest.
Finish	Long and malty.
Comments	Now back in Edrington ownership, a great entry-level malt.
Also try	Aberlour, Glenlivet, Miltonduff
Availability	Specialist retailers
Price	£36 plus

Malt	Glentauchers
Pronounced	*glenn-TOCH-ers*
Distillery	Glentauchers
	Mulben
	KEITH
	AB55 6YL
Owner	Pernod Ricard
Established	1898
Status	In production
Water source	Rosarie Burn
Malt source	Commercial maltsters
Phenols	Unpeated
Casks	Ex-bourbon hogsheads
Capacity	4.2 million litres of alcohol
Stills	Wash: 3 Spirit: 3
Main bottling	15 years old, 40%
Nose	Citrus, nutty, hint of heather honey.
Taste	Ripe berries, caramel and some orange zest, vanilla.
Finish	Long with raisins and chocolate.
Comments	A key malt in the Ballantine's blend.
Also try	Aultmore, Glengoyne, Tamdhu
Availability	Specialist retailers
Price	£44 plus

Malt	Inchgower
Pronounced	*inch-GOW-err*
Distillery	Inchgower
	BUCKIE
	AB56 5AB
Owner	Diageo
Website	www.malts.com
Established	1871
Status	In production
Water source	Springs in the Menduff Hills
Malt source	Burghead Maltings
Phenols	Unpeated
Casks	Refill American oak casks
Capacity	3.2 million litres of alcohol
Stills	Wash: 2 Spirit: 2
Main bottling	Flora & Fauna, 14 years old, 43%
Nose	Rich, deep with faint toffee. Short-crust pastry and fruit.
Taste	Sweet, mouth-drying, with some salt and traces of oil.
Finish	Saccharine-bitter finish that leaves an aftertaste of almonds.
Comments	Interesting post-dinner dram.
Also try	Glenglassaugh, Glentauchers, Tullibardine
Availability	Specialist retailers, independent bottlers
Price	£42 plus

Malt	Kininvie
Pronounced	*kin-INN-vee*
Distillery	Kininvie
	DUFFTOWN
	AB56 4DH
Owner	William Grant & Sons Ltd
Website	www.kininvie.com
Established	1990
Status	In production
Water source	Robbie Dubh Springs
Malt source	Commercial maltsters
Phenols	Unpeated
Casks	Refill ex-bourbon and ex-sherry casks
Capacity	4.8 million litres of alcohol
Stills	Wash: 3 Spirit: 6
Sample	17 years old, 35cl, 42.6%
Nose	Tropical fruits, coconut and vanilla custard, with a hint of milk chocolate.
Taste	Pineapple and mango, linseed oil, ginger and some nuttiness.
Finish	Dries slowly with more linseed oil, spice and soft oak.
Comments	Now producing small-batch experimental expressions as Kininvie Works.
Also try	Glenfiddich, Glen Grant, Glenrothes
Availability	Website, specialist retailers. Has been bottled as Hazelwood.
Price	£35 for the 50cl Kininvie Works releases. £87 for the 17-year-old.

Malt	Knockando
Pronounced	*nock-AAN-doo*
Distillery	Knockando
	KNOCKANDO
	AB38 7RT
Owner	Diageo
Website	www.malts.com
Established	1898
Status	In production
Water source	Cardnach Spring
Malt source	Burghead Maltings
Phenols	Lightly peated
Casks	Refill ex-bourbon hogsheads
Capacity	1.4 million litres of alcohol
Stills	Wash: 2 Spirit: 2
Main bottling	12 years old, 40%
Nose	Fruity-floral, hint of blackcurrant. Water brings up cereal notes and meaty aromas.
Taste	Light-bodied with light mouthfeel, central on the palate. Drying lightly with a trace of acidity.
Finish	Relatively short. Clean and easy to drink.
Comments	A big constituent in J&B blends.
Also try	Aberlour, Glenfarclas, Longmorn
Availability	Specialist retailers
Price	£37 plus

Malt	Linkwood
Distillery	Linkwood
	ELGIN
	IV30 8RD
Owner	Diageo
Website	www.malts.com
Established	1821
Status	In production
Water source	Springs near Millbuies Loch
Malt source	Burghead Maltings
Phenols	Unpeated
Casks	Refill American hogsheads and some refill European butts
Capacity	5.6 million litres of alcohol
Stills	Wash: 3 Spirit: 3
Main bottling	Flora & Fauna, 12 years old, 43%
Nose	Fresh soft-fruits with a hint of vanilla, then light cigar-box notes are perceptible, and a faint hint of expensive ladies' perfume.
Taste	Sweet, viscous, but fresh and clean with pleasant acidity.
Finish	Cedar notes emerge in the finish, which is long.
Comments	Another malt distilled for Diageo's blends.
Also try	Glen Elgin, Glen Grant, Speyside
Availability	Specialist retailers
Price	£40 plus

Malt	**Longmorn**
Distillery	Longmorn
	ELGIN
	IV30 8SJ
Owner	Pernod Ricard
Visitors	By appointment, tel: 01343 554139
Website	www.chivasbrothers.com
Established	1894–5
Status	In production
Water source	Borehole aquifer
Malt source	Commercial maltsters
Phenols	Unpeated
Casks	Ex-bourbon and ex-sherry
Capacity	4.5 million litres of alcohol
Stills	Wash: 4 Spirit: 4
Main bottling	NAS, 40%
Nose	Citrus and toffee sweet. Hints of ginger and spice.
Taste	Creamy with some caramel and chocolate. Hints of orange.
Finish	Medium length. Sweet barley, spicy and oaky.
Comments	A fine, fruity dram.
Also try	Glen Grant, Loch Lomond, Strathisla
Availability	Specialist retailers
Price	£44 plus

Malt	**Macallan**
Pronounced	*mac-AL-an*
Distillery	Macallan
	CRAIGELLACHIE
	AB38 9RX
Owner	Edrington Group
Visitors	Tel: 01340 871471
Website	www.themacallan.com
Established	1824
Status	In production
Water source	Borehole aquifers
Malt source	Simpson's, Berwick-Upon-Tweed
Phenols	Unpeated
Casks	First-fill and refill ex-sherry Spanish and American oak, some ex-bourbon
Capacity	15 million litres of alcohol
Stills	Wash: 12 Spirit: 24
Sample	Double Cask, 12 years old, 40%
Nose	Christmas cake dried fruit and sherry.
Taste	Smooth with honey and orange peel, spice and baked patisserie.
Finish	Dried fruits with vanilla and a hint of wood spice.
Comments	A bewildering range of expressions is now available.
Also try	GlenDronach, Mortlach, Dalmore
Availability	Everywhere
Price	£42 plus

Malt	Mannochmore
Pronounced	*man-OCH-more*
Distillery	Mannochmore
	ELGIN
	IV30 8SS
Owner	Diageo
Website	www.malts.com
Established	1971
Status	In production
Water source	Bardon Burn
Malt source	Burghead Maltings
Phenols	Lightly peated
Casks	Refill American hogsheads
Capacity	6 million litres of alcohol
Stills	Wash: 3 Spirit: 3
Main bottling	Flora & Fauna, 12 years old, 43%
Nose	Light with fragrant orange citrus.
Taste	Sweet, floral, zesty, with vanilla and a hint of mint.
Finish	Medium, refreshing with a hint of almond.
Comments	Glenlossie's sister distillery. Good aperitif dram.
Also try	Auchentoshan, Glenlossie, Glen Spey
Availability	Specialist retailers
Price	£33 plus

Malt	Miltonduff
Distillery	Miltonduff
	ELGIN
	IV30 8TQ
Owner	Pernod Ricard
Established	1824
Status	In production
Water source	Borehole aquifer
Malt source	Commercial maltsters
Phenols	Unpeated
Casks	Refill and first-fill American oak
Capacity	5.8 million litres of alcohol
Stills	Wash: 3 Spirit: 3
Main bottling	15 years old, 40%
Nose	Floral with peaches, vanilla, dried fruit.
Taste	Peach, orange, some creamy chocolate and baked dough.
Finish	Long, satisfying, with honey hints and some spice.
Comments	Until 1981 Mosstowie malt was also produced at Miltonduff in Lomond stills.
Also try	Tomatin, Teaninich, Knockando
Availability	Specialist retailers
Price	£38 plus

Malt	**Mortlach**
Distillery	Mortlach
	DUFFTOWN
	AB55 4AQ
Owner	Diageo
Website	www.mortlach.com
Established	1823
Status	In production
Water source	Local springs
Malt source	Burghead Maltings
Phenols	Unpeated
Casks	Refill Ex-bourbon and ex-sherry
Capacity	3.8 million litres of alcohol
Stills	Wash: 3 Spirit: 3
Main bottling	12 years old, 40%
Nose	Rich and deep. A balance of oak and sandalwood. Light spice, charred toffee and red berries.
Taste	Medium- to full-bodied mouthfeel. Sweet and spicy. Notes of demerara sugar, dark chocolate, cherry jam, light tobacco. Meaty.
Finish	Smooth and dry, with bitter plums.
Comments	First-class after-dinner malt, relaunched in 2018 and almost triple-distilled.
Also try	Cragganmore, Macallan, Benrinnes
Availability	Specialist retailers
Price	£44 plus

Malt	The Singleton of Dufftown
Distillery	Dufftown DUFFTOWN AB55 4ER
Owner	Diageo
Website	www.malts.com
Established	1896
Status	In production
Water source	Jock's Well in the Conval Hills
Malt source	Burghead Maltings
Phenols	Unpeated
Casks	Ex-bourbon and sherry refills
Capacity	6 million litres of alcohol
Stills	Wash: 3 Spirit: 3
Main bottling	12 years old, 40%
Nose	Sweet malt and cereals. Toast and nuts.
Taste	Citrus, nuts and toffee with grassy hints.
Finish	Full, oaky with lingering fruit.
Comments	A major component in Bell's Original blend.
Also try	Glenfiddich, Glen Spey, Speyburn
Availability	Everywhere
Price	£34 plus

Malt	The Singleton of Glendullan
Distillery	Glendullan DUFFTOWN AB55 4DJ
Owner	Diageo
Visitors	By appointment, tel: 01340 822100
Website	www.thesingleton.com
Established	1897–8
Status	In production
Water source	Springs in the Conval Hills
Malt source	Burghead Maltings
Phenols	Unpeated
Casks	Ex-bourbon refill hogsheads and some European oak
Capacity	5 million litres of alcohol
Stills	Wash: 3 Spirit: 3
Main bottling	12 years old, 75cl, 40%
Nose	Fresh, light and clean. Fresh fruitiness and soft fragrant notes; scented leather, subtle sandalwood and vanilla.
Taste	Light to medium. Fresh and easy to drink; spicy, then soft and sweet. Fruity, with citrus, raisins, vanilla and a hint of honey.
Finish	Short, creamy and smooth.
Comments	More likely to be found in export markets and at the distillery. Also as the House of Tully, Game of Thrones expression.
Also try	Glenfiddich, Balvenie, Glenlivet
Availability	Global retail travel, specialist retailers
Price	£38 plus

Malt	Speyburn
Distillery	Speyburn
	ABERLOUR
	AB38 7AG
Owner	Inver House Distillers Ltd
Website	www.speyburn.com
Established	1897
Status	In production
Water source	Granty Burn sourced on the western slope of the Glen of Rothes
Malt source	Commercial maltsters
Phenols	Unpeated
Casks	Ex-bourbon casks
Capacity	4.5 million litres of alcohol
Stills	Wash: 1 Spirit: 1
Main bottling	10 years old, 40%
Nose	Fresh, clean and aromatic with a rich lemony fruitiness.
Taste	Medium bodied with hints of toffee and butterscotch.
Finish	Long and sweet.
Comments	One of the five malts from the Inver House stable. A beautifully located distillery.
Also try	Pittyvaich, Glen Spey, Longmorn
Availability	Specialist retailers
Price	£25 plus

Malt	**Strathisla**
Pronounced	*strath-EYE-la*
Distillery	Strathisla
	KEITH
	AB55 5BS
Owner	Pernod Ricard
Visitors	Tel: 01542 783044
Website	www.chivas.com
Established	1786
Status	In production
Water source	Broomhill and Newmill Spring
Malt source	Paul's Malt of Buckie
Phenols	Unpeated
Casks	First-fill and refill ex-bourbon
Capacity	2.45 million litres of alcohol
Stills	Wash: 2 Spirit: 2
Main bottling	12 years old, 40%
Nose	Rich and fruity with a complex array of haylike aromas balanced with a dry oakiness.
Taste	Full, fruity and hay-like flavours with a mellow nutty sweetness.
Finish	Rich and mellow.
Comments	A striking, romantic-looking distillery.
Also try	Aberfeldy, Cragganmore, Longmorn
Availability	Specialist retailers
Price	£33 plus

Malt	Strathmill
Pronounced	*strath-MILL*
Distillery	Strathmill
	KEITH
	AB55 5DQ
Owner	Diageo
Website	www.malts.com
Established	1891
Status	In production
Water source	Local springs
Malt source	Burghead Maltings
Phenols	Unpeated
Casks	Refill hogsheads and ex-sherry butts
Capacity	2.6 million litres of alcohol
Stills	Wash: 2 Spirit: 2
Main bottling	Flora & Fauna, 12 years old, 43%
Nose	Closed at full strength, with a hint of 'Café Noir' biscuits.
Taste	Smooth, with a medium body. Sweet start. Some acidity.
Finish	A medium-length, dry finish. Chocolaty aftertaste.
Comments	One of the principal malts used in the J&B blend.
Also try	Pittyvaich, Oban, Tamnavulin
Availability	Rare. Specialist retailers, independent bottlers
Price	£36 plus

Malt	Stronachie
Pronounced	*stron-a-key*
Distillery	Benrinnes
	ABERLOUR
	AB38 9NN
Owner	AD Rattray Ltd
Website	www.adrattray.com
Established	c.1826
Status	In production
Water source	Rowantree and Scurran burns
Malt source	Burghead and Roseisle Maltings
Phenols	Unpeated
Casks	Mainly European oak
Capacity	3.5 million litres of alcohol
Stills	Wash: 2 Spirit: 4
Main bottling	10 years old, 43%
Nose	Soft honey, earthy heather and malty sweetness.
Taste	Smooth with honey and biscuits, then lingering pepper and cereal notes.
Finish	Balanced and satisfying.
Comments	This unique malt is a close match to the 1904 bottling of Stronachie in Kinross-shire which closed in the 1920s.
Also try	Benrinnes, Cragganmore, Scapa
Availability	Website, specialist retailers
Price	£33 plus

Malt	Tamdhu
Pronounced	*taam-DOO*
Distillery	Tamdhu
	ABERLOUR
	AB38 7RP
Owner	Ian Macleod Distillers Ltd
Website	www.tamdhu.com
Established	1896–7
Status	In production
Water source	Borehole and springs beneath the distillery
Malt source	Crisp and Simpsons
Phenols	Unpeated
Casks	Refill ex-sherry Oloroso and American oak, some ex-bourbon
Capacity	4 million litres of alcohol
Stills	Wash: 3 Spirit: 3
Main bottling	12 years old, 43%
Nose	Rich, iced cinnamon rolls, orange boiled sweets, fresh sweet oak with raisins and the faint hint of mint.
Taste	Silky texture that coats the mouth with banana, berry jam, malt biscuit and sherry-oak depth.
Finish	Long and balanced with ground spice, dried fruit and soft Scottish tablet – finally unveiling a wisp of peat smoke.
Comments	A revitalised Speyside dram.
Also try	Benromach, Benrinnes, GlenDronach
Availability	Specialist retailers
Price	£34 plus

Malt	**Tamnavulin**
Pronounced	*tamna-VOOL-inn*
Distillery	Tamnavulin
	BALLINDALLOCH
	AB37 9JA
Owner	Whyte & Mackay Ltd
Website	www.tamnavulinwhisky.com
Established	1966
Status	In production
Water source	Local springs
Malt source	Commercial maltsters
Phenols	Trace
Casks	First-fill ex-bourbon and ex-sherry
Capacity	4 million litres of alcohol
Stills	Wash: 3 Spirit: 3
Main bottling	Double Cask, NAS, 40%
Nose	Rich, warm aromas of apple, toffee and honey with sweet marzipan and subtle tangy marmalade notes.
Taste	Fresh, mellow with pear creamy peaches and pineapple and a hint of Demerara sugar.
Finish	Rich, smooth and refreshing.
Comments	A blending malt used in Whyte & Mackay, now gaining more recognition.
Also try	Benromach, Craigellachie, Teaninich
Availability	Widespread
Price	£33 plus

Malt	Tomintoul
Pronounced	*tommin-TOWEL*
Distillery	Tomintoul BALLINDALLOCH AB37 9AQ
Owner	Angus Dundee Distillers plc
Website	www.angusdundee.co.uk
Established	1964–5
Status	In production
Water source	Ballantruan Spring
Malt source	Commercial maltsters
Phenols	Unpeated
Casks	Refill and first-fill hogsheads and some Oloroso ex-sherry butts
Capacity	3.3 million litres of alcohol
Stills	Wash: 2 Spirit: 2
Main bottling	10 years old, 40%
Nose	Suggestions of citrus, toffee tones with a hint of raisins.
Taste	Clean, creamy, light-bodied – some sweetness balanced by gentle oaky spice.
Finish	Long with sweetness followed by spice.
Comments	Known as 'the gentle dram' understandably. Now available in a myriad of interesting expressions.
Also try	Bladnoch, Glenkinchie, Glen Moray
Availability	Widespread
Price	£28 plus

Malt	Tormore
Distillery	Tormore
	GRANTOWN-ON-SPEY
	PH26 3LR
Owner	Pernod Ricard
Established	1958–60
Website	www.tormoredistillery.com
Status	In production
Water source	Achvochkie Burn
Malt source	Commercial maltsters
Phenols	Unpeated
Casks	Refill ex-bourbon casks
Capacity	4.8 million litres of alcohol
Stills	Wash: 4 Spirit: 4
Main bottling	14 years old, 43%
Nose	Citrus, raspberry and toasted almonds and a hint of spice.
Taste	Creamy toffee and vanilla, liquorice and ginger.
Finish	Long and sweet with a spicy, peppery tang.
Comments	An unique-looking distillery.
Also try	Deanston, Tomintoul, Glenfiddich
Availability	Widespread
Price	£49 plus

The Highlands

FOUR distinct producing regions exist around Speyside at all points of the compass. In the north the activity ranges from Dalwhinnie to Wolfburn by way of recently commissioned Ardross and Toulvaddie, which is still in construction. In all 16 active distilleries exist in this area and will soon be joined by a reinstated Brora. The sparser western Highlands contain Oban, Nc'nean, Ardnamurchan and Ben Nevis while in the south nine distilleries extend from Loch Lomond and Glengoyne on the edge of the Lowlands to Edradour, which marks the upper boundary in Perthshire. The east consist largely of Aberdeen and Angus-based distilleries with 11 active distilleries such as Ardmore, Knockdhu, Glencadam, and the newly established Brew Dog and Arbikie. The total number of active Highland malt distilleries numbers 37 (Invergordon grain distillery is also based in the northern region).

In the southern Highlands Glenturret's association with The Famous Grouse blend has ended as Edrington has divested ownership to the Lalique Group which is revamping the operation. The Loch Lomond Group, owners of Loch Lomond and Glen Scotia in Campbeltown, was surprisingly sold in 2019 to Hillhouse Capital Management. In the same year the tiny Perthshire Strathearn farm distillery was acquired by Douglas Laing & Co, the Glasgow-based independent bottlers.

To the east Arbikie, near Montrose, has undertaken some early experimentation in distilling rye whisky which was released in 2018. BrewDog (previously Lone Wolf) in Ellon has also distilled rye whisky and a 50-litre pot still is used for experimentation with new styles. Twin River near Banchory, later renamed Deeside Distillery, has come and gone but, partly funded from the proceeds of the sale of 88 of its 100 casks, a new larger distillery is planned.

GlenWyvis near Dingwall has emerged from rounds of local funding as a community-led distillery with more plans to expand. Further north Dornoch is a tiny distillery which

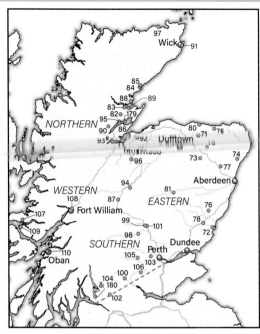

Distillery number refers to page number.

produces a large range of spirits under the auspices of the Thompson family, owners of the adjoining Dornoch Castle Hotel. Wolfburn, near Thurso, is Scotland's most northerly mainland distillery and is now producing a large range of malt whisky and is to be joined by another micro-distillery at John o'Groats which has just received planning approval.

In the west Nc'nean, situated on the stunning Drimnin estate over the water from Tobermory, is now up and running. Since 2000, nine new distilleries have emerged in the Highlands and there are another two either at the planning stage or in construction.

The northern and western Highland malts are generally robust in nature with some maritime hints while the eastern and southern malts display more subtle characteristics which help master blenders to create some of the most popular Scotch whiskies.

Malt	anCnoc
Pronounced	*a-NOCK*
Distillery	Knockdhu
	by HUNTLY
	AB54 7LJ
Owner	Inver House Distillers Ltd
Visitors	By appointment, tel: 01466 771223
Website	www.ancnoc.com
Established	1893-4
Status	In production
Water source	Four springs on the Knock Hill
Malt source	Local commercial maltsters
Phenols	Unpeated
Casks	Ex-bourbon and ex-sherry casks
Capacity	2 million litres of alcohol
Stills	Wash: 1 Spirit: 1
Main bottling	12 years old, 40%
Nose	Soft, very aromatic with a hint of honey and lemon in the foreground.
Taste	Sweet to start with an appetising fruitiness.
Finish	Long and smooth. A malt for every occasion.
Comments	An award-winning malt from the Inver House stable.
Also try	Knockando, Arran, Loch Lomond
Availability	Specialist retailers
Price	£30 plus

Grain	Arbikie
Pronounced	*arr-bee-kee*
Distillery	Arbikie
	Inverkeilor
	ARBROATH
	DD11 4UZ
Owner	Arbikie Distilling Ltd
Website	www.arbikie.com
Established	2015
Status	In production
Water source	Deep well under the distillery
Grain source	Own-estate conditioned at Boortmalt, Montrose.
Phenols	Unpeated
Casks	Rye matured in first-fill charred American oak and Armagnac barrels. Whisky will be matured in ex-bourbon and ex-sherry.
Capacity	200,000 litres of alcohol
Stills	Wash: 1 Spirit: 1 Gin: 1
Sample	4 years old, 46%, Release No 2
Nose	Dark cacao, pipe tobacco, old spice, cloves.
Taste	Dates, apricot, caraway.
Finish	Muscular with spice and brown sugar.
Comments	Rye mash bill consists of 52% unmalted Arantes Scottish rye, 33% unmalted Viscount Scottish wheat, 15% Odyssey Scottish malted barley. The first rye whisky to be distilled in Scotland in over 100 years. Malt whisky release expected 2029/2030.
Availability	Website and specialist retailers
Price	£250

Malt	Ardmore
Pronounced	*ard-MOOR*
Distillery	Ardmore
	KENNETHMONT
	AB54 4NH
Owner	Beam Suntory
Website	www.ardmorewhisky.com
Established	1899
Status	In production
Water source	15 springs on Knockandy Hill
Malt source	Commercial maltsters
Phenols	12–14 ppm
Casks	European oak, ex-bourbon and first-fill quarter casks.
Capacity	5.55 million litres of alcohol
Stills	Wash: 4 Spirit: 4
Main bottling	NAS, 40%
Nose	Heather Honey with hints of cinnamon, toffee bonbon and peat smoke.
Taste	Creamy vanilla spice gives way to smoky charcoal notes, especially with a dash of water, balanced by sweet honey and spice.
Finish	Full-bodied, silky mouthfeel with a dry, tangy and lingering aftertaste, coupled with spice notes.
Comments	A rare beast on Speyside ... a peated malt.
Also try	Glen Scotia, Bowmore, Loch Lomond
Availability	Everywhere
Price	£30 plus

Malt	BrewDog
Distillery	BrewDog
	Balmacassie Commercial Park
	ELLON
	AB41 8BR
Owner	Brewdog Distilling Co
Visitors	Tel: 01358 724 924
Website	www.brewdog.com
Established	2016
Status	In production
Water source	Mains supply
Grain source	Simpson's and Crisp Malt
Phenols	Unpeated
Casks	Ex-Bourbon, toasted virgin oak, ex-Oloroso and PX sherry, French oak and STR.
Capacity	450,000 litres of alcohol
Stills	Wash: 1 Spirit: 1 Gin: 1
Sample	Skeleton Key, 46%
Nose	Freshly cut grass, green apples and brown sugar, hidden beneath waves of smoke.
Taste	Notes of oat and honey cookies, sharp citrus and a whisper of peat smoke, as well as salty sea-breeze.
Finish	Zesty, with that hint of sea salt and smoke.
Comments	BrewDog is bottling Zuidam Dutch rye whisky and Skeleton Key, a blend not distilled at Ellon, with Duncan Taylor Ltd of Huntly. The temperature and humidity controlled warehouse can mimic various maturation environments.
Also try	Arbikie, Wolfburn, GlenWyvis
Availability	Website and specialist retailers
Price	£32 plus

Malt	The Deveron
Distillery	Macduff
	MACDUFF
	AB45 3JT
Owner	John Dewar & Sons Ltd
Website	www.TheDeveron.com
Established	1960
Status	In production
Water source	Local springs
Malt source	Commercial maltsters
Phenols	Unpeated
Casks	Refill and first-fill hogsheads and butts
Capacity	3.4 million litres of alcohol
Stills	Wash: 2 Spirit: 3
Main bottling	12 years old, 40%
Nose	Hints of vanilla, touch of honey. After adding some water there are hints of almond and creamy oak.
Taste	Chocolate-coated almonds, vine fruits, dusty grains and spices. Medium-bodied with sherried notes.
Finish	Dry, lightly spiced.
Comments	The range was relaunched in 2015 with new packaging and a change of name from Glen Deveron.
Also try	Banff, Auchroisk, Glenglassaugh
Availability	Specialist retailers
Price	£32 plus

Malt	Fettercairn
Distillery	Fettercairn
	LAURENCEKIRK
	AB30 1YB
Owner	Whyte & Mackay Ltd
Visitors	Tel: 01561 340205
Webste	www.fettercairnwhisky.com
Established	1824
Status	In production
Water source	Springs in the Grampians
Malt source	Commercial maltsters
Phenols	Up to 15 ppm
Casks	Ex-bourbon and ex-sherry
Capacity	3.2 million litres of alcohol
Stills	Wash: 2 Spirit: 2
Main bottling	NAS, 42%
Nose	Tropical fruits and spices.
Taste	The fruit remains with nectarine, subtle roasted coffee, clove, and ginger.
Finish	Vanilla and pear, with soft spices.
Comments	A revamped range that deserves investigation.
Also try	Deanston, Ardmore, Tormore
Availability	Specialist retailers
Price	£46 plus

Malt	Glen Garioch
Pronounced	*glen GEE-REE*
Distillery	Glen Garioch
	OLDMELDRUM
	AB51 0ES
Owner	Beam Suntory
Visitors	Tel: 01651 873450
Website	www.glengarioch.com
Established	1797
Status	In production
Water source	Springs on Percock Hill
Malt source	Simpson's, Berwick-Upon-Tweed
Phenols	Unpeated
Casks	Ex-bourbon and sherry
Capacity	1.37 million litres of alcohol
Stills	Wash: 1 Spirit: 1
Main bottling	Founder's Reserve, NAS, 48%
Nose	Sweet vanilla and spice combine with green apple and grapefruit.
Taste	Butter cream and vanilla then green apple skin and citrus.
Finish	Zesty and refreshing.
Comments	One of Scotland's oldest distilleries.
Also try	Oban, Craigellachie, Glenury Royal
Availability	Specialist retailers
Price	£35 plus

Malt	**Glencadam**
Distillery	Glencadam
	BRECHIN
	DD9 7PA
Owner	Angus Dundee Distillers plc
Visitors	By appointment, tel: 01356 622217
Website	www.glencadamwhisky.com
Established	1825
Status	In production
Water source	Loch Lee
Malt source	Commercial maltsters
Phenols	Unpeated
Casks	Ex-bourbon and ex-sherry
Capacity	1.3 million litres of alcohol
Stills	Wash: 1 Spirit: 1
Main bottling	Origin 1825, NAS, 46%
Nose	Creamy, floral malted barley with hints of vanilla and mixed summer fruits.
Taste	Bananas, pineapple, pears and boiled sweets merge with a mix of soft spice.
Finish	Floral with pear-drop sweetness.
Comments	Brechin's last remaining distillery.
Also try	Glenesk, North Port, Lochside
Availability	Specialist retailers
Price	£26 plus

Malt	GlenDronach
Pronounced	*glen-DRONN-ach*
Distillery	GlenDronach
	FORGUE
	AB54 6DB
Owner	Brown Forman
Visitors	Tel: 01466 730202
Website	www.glendronachdistillery.co.uk
Established	1826
Status	In production
Water source	Dronac Burn
Malt source	Commercial maltsters
Phenols	Lightly peated
Casks	Ex-bourbon and ex-sherry
Capacity	1.4 million litres of alcohol
Stills	Wash: 2 Spirit: 2
Main bottling	15 years old, 40%
Nose	Orange blossom and citrus twist with buttery, golden sultanas, sun-dried raisins and ripe yellow plums. A touch of vanilla.
Taste	Crisp oak spices, soaked sultanas, apricot jam and gingerbread. Delicate hints of butterscotch, cocoa and toasted almonds.
Finish	Sherried, refined, complex.
Comments	A much extended range which will appeal to after-dinner drammers.
Also try	Dalmore, Macallan, Mortlach
Availability	Widespread
Price	£37 plus

Malt	Glenglassaugh
Pronounced	*glen-GLASS-aa*
Distillery	Glenglassaugh PORTSOY AB45 2SQ
Owner	BenRiach Distillery Co
Visitors	Seasonal. Tel: 0131 335 5135
Website	www.glenglassaugh.com
Established	1875
Status	In production
Water source	Wells near the Glassaugh Spring
Malt source	Commercial maltsters
Phenols	Unpeated
Casks	Ex-bourbon, refill hogsheads and ex-sherry butts
Capacity	1.1 million litres of alcohol
Stills	Wash: 1 Spirit: 1
Main bottling	Revival, NAS, 46%
Nose	Sweet caramel and toffee with notes of nutty sherry, milk chocolate and honey. Ripe plums, red berries and oranges. Caramelised sugar and earthy, charred oak.
Taste	Sweet, rounded and creamy. Oranges, plums, cherry and walnuts, chocolate, honey-mead, sherry and soft, spiced oak.
Finish	Medium with warming mulled-wine spices, sherry and caramel.
Comments	A much extended range with something for everyone.
Also try	GlenDronach, The Deveron, Inchgower
Availability	Specialist retailers
Price	£37 plus

Malt	Royal Lochnagar
Distillery	Royal Lochnagar
	BALLATER
	AB35 5TB
Owner	Diageo
Visitors	Tel: 01339 742700
Website	www.malts.com
Established	1845
Status	In production
Water source	Springs beneath the distillery
Malt source	Roseisle Maltings
Phenols	Unpeated
Casks	American oak and European ex-sherry
Capacity	500,000 litres of alcohol
Stills	Wash: 1 Spirit: 1
Main bottling	12 years old, 40%
Nose	Planed wood, light toffee, boat varnish. After a while, coffee with brown sugar.
Taste	Medium-bodied. Pleasant, an initial sweetness is quickly overtaken by acidity.
Finish	Dry, medium-length, with an attractive lingering sandalwood aftertaste.
Comments	Queen Victoria's favourite tipple.
Also try	anCnoc, Aberfeldy, Glen Elgin
Availability	Widespread
Price	£35 plus

Malt	**Ardross**
Distillery	Ardross
	Ardross Mains
	ALNESS
	IV17 0YE
Owner	Greenwood Distillers Ltd
Website	www.greenwooddistillers.com
Established	2019
Status	In production
Water source	Loch Dubh
Malt source	Not known
Phenols	Not known
Casks	Not known
Capacity	1 million litres of alcohol
Stills	Wash: 1 Spirit: 1 Gin: 1
Comments	No new make tasting sample available. Very recently commissioned but already selling Theodore Pictish gin distilled (illustrated) in an old Charentais alambic.

Malt	Balblair
Distillery	Balblair
	TAIN
	IV19 1LB
Owner	Inver House Distillers Ltd
Visitors	Tel: 01862 821273
Website	www.balblair.com
Established	1790
Status	In production
Water source	Allt Dearg Burn
Malt source	Portgordon Maltings
Phenols	Unpeated
Casks	First- and second-fill ex-bourbon and refill ex-sherry
Capacity	1.8 million litres of alcohol
Stills	Wash: 1 Spirit: 1
Main bottling	12 years old, 46%
Nose	Bright lemon peel layered with creamy vanilla and crisp green apples.
Taste	Ground spices and dried orange slices with set honey sweetness.
Finish	Creamy, leathery with notes of sweet vanilla.
Comments	A revamped, age-statement range.
Also try	Glenmorangie, Aultmore, Old Pulteney
Availability	Widespread
Price	£44 plus

Malt	Brora
Pronounced	*BROAR-ah*
Distillery	Brora
	BRORA
	KW9 6LR
Owner	Diageo
Website	www.malts.com
Established	1819. Closed 1983
Status	Under reconstruction in 2020
Water source	Clyne Burn
Malt source	Not known
Phenols	Not known
Casks	Refill American and European oak casks
Capacity	800,000 litres of alcohol
Stills	Wash: 1 Spirit: 1
Sample	Limited Edition, 35 years old, 48.6%
Nose	Subtle, dry salt in an old-fashioned canvas tent with juicy fruit compote.
Taste	Light sweetness, ripe autumn fruits, salty, with smoke behind, then chocolate cake.
Finish	Peppery-hot, tongue-tingling and sharply warming. Drying, supple oak with cinnamon, mint and pine resin give over to a memory of the coast: distant sand, fresh ozone and smoke.
Comments	Rare and very expensive. A remarkable coastal Highland malt.
Also try	Old Pulteney, Bowmore, Ledaig
Availability	Website, specialist retailers and independent bottlers.
Price	£1,500 plus

Malt	Clynelish
Pronounced	*klyne-leesh*
Distillery	Clynelish
	BRORA
	KW9 6LR
Owner	Diageo
Visitors	Tel: 01408 623003
Website	www.malts.com
Established	1967
Status	In production
Water source	Clynemilton Burn
Malt source	Glen Ord Maltings
Phenols	Unpeated
Casks	Ex-bourbon and ex-sherry
Capacity	4.8 million litres of alcohol
Stills	Wash: 3 Spirit: 3
Main bottling	14 years old, 46%
Nose	Light candle wax with some sugar, faint floral fragrance.
Taste	Pleasant, creamy mouthfeel with maritime overtones. Light to medium-bodied.
Finish	Some salt, dryish yet an attractive, even slightly bitter finish.
Comments	Next door to Brora yet utterly different.
Also try	Balblair, Glenmorangie, Glen Elgin
Availability	Website, specialist retailers
Price	£45 plus

Malt	Dalmore
Pronounced	*daal-moor*
Distillery	Dalmore
	ALNESS
	IV17 0UT
Owner	Whyte & Mackay Ltd
Visitors	Tel: 01349 882362
Website	www.thedalmore.com
Established	1839
Status	In production
Water source	Loch Kildermorie
Malt source	Bairds of Inverness
Phenols	Unpeated
Casks	Ex-bourbon and ex-sherry
Capacity	4.3 million litres of alcohol
Stills	Wash: 4 Spirit: 4
Main bottling	12 years old, 40%
Nose	Citrus fruits, chocolate and aromatic spices.
Taste	Seville oranges, dried fruits and hints of vanilla pod.
Finish	Roasted coffee and dark chocolate.
Comments	A magnificent post-dinner malt.
Also try	Dailuaine, Macallan, GlenDronach
Availability	Widespread
Price	£43 plus

Malt	Dalwhinnie
Pronounced	*daal-whinn-ay*
Distillery	Dalwhinnie
	DALWHINNIE
	PH19 1AA
Owner	Diageo
Visitors.	Tel: 01540 672219
Website	www.malts.com
Established	1897
Status	In production
Water source	Allt an t'Sluie Burn
Malt source	Roseisle Maltings
Phenols	Lightly peated
Casks	Ex-bourbon, matured offsite in central Scotland
Capacity	2.2 million litres of alcohol
Stills	Wash: 1 Spirit: 1
Main bottling	15 years old, 43%
Nose	Big, crisp, dry and very aromatic with hints of heather and peat.
Taste	Heather-honey sweetness and vanilla followed by deeper citrus fruit and hints of malted bread.
Finish	Long, lingering, surprisingly intense; starts sweetly, then gives way to smoke, peat and malt.
Comments	Scotland's highest distillery (356 m/1168 ft)
Also try	Balvenie, Glenlivet, Linkwood
Availability	Everywhere
Price	£36 plus

Malt	Dornoch
Distillery	Dornoch
	Castle Close
	DORNOCH
	IV25 3SD
Owner	Dornoch Distillery Co
Visitors	By appointment, tel: 01862 810216
Website	www.dornochdistillery.com
Established	2016
Status	In production
Water source	Mains supply
Malt source	Warminster floor maltings, heritage varieties
Phenols	Unpeated
Casks	First-fill and refill American oak
Capacity	30,000 litres of alcohol
Stills	Wash: 1 Spirit: 1 Gin: 1
Main bottling	New make, 20cl, 60%
Nose	Clean and slightly coastal, pears, and greengages, hints of ripe melon and pink peppercorns.
Taste	Waxy with a hit of pepper, salty with blueberry and raspberry. Water brings out candyfloss and lychee.
Finish	Long and aromatic with pink peppercorns and stone fruits.
Comments	Innovative distilling promises much for the future at Dornoch.
Also try	Nc'nean, Ardnamurchan, BrewDog
Availability	Specialist retailers
Price	£15 plus

Malt	Glenmorangie
Pronounced	*glen-MOR-anjay*
Distillery	Glenmorangie
	TAIN
	IV19 1PZ
Owner	LVMH
Visitors	Tel: 01862 892477
Website	www.glenmorangie.com
Established	1843
Status	In production
Water source	Tarlogie Springs
Malt source	Commercial maltsters
Phenols	Unpeated
Casks	First and second refill ex-bourbon with some other woods for finishing
Capacity	6.2 million litres of alcohol
Stills	Wash: 6 Spirit: 6
Main bottling	10 years old, 40%
Nose	The scent of citrus and ripening peaches is softened by the aroma of vanilla.
Taste	Vanilla first which brings a burst of flowery fruitiness.
Finish	Lingering notes of orange and peach.
Comments	A very popular malt, particularly in Scotland.
Also try	Glen Elgin, Glen Grant, anCnoc
Availability	Everywhere
Price	£33 plus

Malt	GlenWyvis
Pronounced	*glen-WI-viss*
Distillery	Upper Dochcarty
	DINGWALL
	IV15 9UF
Owner	GlenWyvis Distillery Ltd
Visitors	By appointment, tel: 01349 862005
Website	www.glenwyvis.com
Established	2017
Status	In production
Water source	Borehole aquifer
Malt source	Bairds
Phenols	Unpeated
Casks	American oak
Capacity	140,000 litres of alcohol
Stills	Wash: 1 Spirit: 1 Gin: 1
Sample	NAS, 46%
Nose	Vanilla, toffee, fudge and some subtle peach with a little malt barley.
Taste	Caramel, citrus, marzipan, fresh apricot and sweet honey. A dash of water brings out more of the creamy vanilla and a buttery feel.
Finish	The sweetness fades and leaves a refreshing and clean taste reminiscent of a freshly sliced fruit salad.
Comments	This expression is from an unnamed Highland distillery.
Availability	Distillery and specialist retailers
Price	£47

Malt	Old Pulteney
Pronounced	*old POOLT-nay*
Distillery	Pulteney
	Huddart Street
	WICK
	KW1 5BA
Owner	Inver House Distillers Ltd
Visitors	Tel: 01955 602371
Website	www.oldpulteney.com
Established	1826
Status	In production
Water source	Mains water from the Loch of Hempriggs
Phenols	Unpeated
Casks	Ex-bourbon and ex-sherry
Capacity	1.8 million litres of alcohol
Stills	Wash: 1 Spirit: 1
Main bottling	12 years old, 40%
Nose	Medium to high intensity, dry with a hint of sea air.
Taste	Dry, medium-bodied and smooth, redolent of honey and cream, faintly salty with a slight spicy note.
Finish	Sweet and lingering.
Comments	Popular dram from the once dry town of Wick.
Also try	Oban, Glen Garioch, Tomatin
Availability	Everywhere
Price	£29 plus

Malt	**Royal Brackla**
Distillery	Royal Brackla
	Cawdor
	NAIRN
	IV12 5QY
Owner	John Dewar & Sons Ltd
Website	www.RoyalBrackla.com
Established	c.1812
Status	In production
Water source	Cursack Springs
Malt source	Commercial maltsters
Phenols	Unpeated
Casks	Refill American oak casks and ex-Oloroso sherry
Capacity	4.1 million litres of alcohol
Stills	Wash: 2 Spirit: 2
Main bottling	12 years old, 40%
Nose	Spices in warm malt and peaches.
Taste	Spice and smoky soft fruit against notes of sherried sweetness.
Finish	Long with citrus fruit, slice and cocoa.
Comments	The new core range was launched in 2015.
Also try	GlenDronach, Benromach, Cardhu
Availability	Specialist retailers
Price	£46 plus

Malt	The Singleton of Glen Ord
Distillery	Glen Ord
	MUIR OF ORD
	IV6 7UJ
Owner	Diageo
Visitors	Tel: 01463 872004
Website	www.malts.com
Established	1838
Status	In production
Water source	Nan Eun and Nam Bonnach lochs
Malt source	Glen Ord Maltings
Phenols	Lightly peated
Casks	Fresh and refill ex-sherry butts and refill hogsheads
Capacity	11 million litres of alcohol
Stills	Wash: 7 Spirit: 7
Main bottling	12 years old, 40%
Nose	Winey top notes rapidly evolve into plummy fruits offset by zesty, oily orange peel. Then, rich caramel toffees, chocolate and malty biscuits.
Taste	Light- to medium-bodied, coating mouthfeel with a balance of gentle fruit tartness and gingery, rich, sweet malt. Becoming lighter and cleaner on the palate.
Finish	Balance of lightly cleansing fruit notes and gingery toasted maltiness; a smooth texture, like good chocolate slowly melting on the tongue.
Comments	Primarily found abroad but also available direct from the distillery.
Also try	BenRiach, Glen Elgin, Royal Brackla
Availability	Distillery and specialist retailers
Price	£30 plus

Malt	**Spey Tenné**
Distillery	Speyside
	Glen Tromie
	KINGUSSIE
	PH21 1NS
Owner	Harvey's of Edinburgh International
Visitors	By appointment, tel: 01540 661060
Website	www.speysidedistillery.co.uk
Established	1990
Status	In production
Water source	River Tromie
Malt source	Local commercial maltsters
Phenols	Less than 5ppm
Casks	Refill ex-bourbon, ex-sherry and ex-port
Capacity	600,000 litres of alcohol
Stills	Wash: 1　Spirit: 1　Gin: 1
Main bottling	NAS, 46%
Nose	Medium, fruity overall with a faded hint of pot-pourri.
Taste	Light texture, sweet and faintly fruity, then drying slightly. Becomes sweeter with water.
Finish	Light, fruity, sweet.
Comments	An anytime malt now revamped and relaunched.
Also try	Glen Grant, Knockando, Loch Lomond
Availability	Specialist retailers
Price	£37 plus

Malt	Teaninich
Pronounced	*tee-ninn-ich*
Distillery	Teaninich
	ALNESS
	IV17 0XB
Owner	Diageo
Website	www.malts.com
Established	1817
Status	In production
Water source	Dairywell Spring
Malt source	Glen Ord Maltings
Phenols	Unpeated
Casks	Refill ex-bourbon hogsheads with some ex-sherry butts
Capacity	10.2 million litres of alcohol
Stills	Wash: 6 Spirit: 6
Main bottling	Flora & Fauna, 10 years old, 43%
Nose	Fresh and citric, a scent of violets, orange juice and old oranges.
Taste	Light to medium body, crisp and zesty. Light and sweetish, but overall dry with acidity and a pinch of salt.
Finish	Long and dry with beeswax.
Comments	Now one of Diageo's largest malt distilleries.
Also try	Balblair, Royal Brackla, Old Pulteney
Availability	Website, specialist retailers
Price	£30 plus

Malt	Tomatin
Pronounced	*tom-AA-tin*
Distillery	Tomatin
	TOMATIN
	IV13 7YT
Owner	Takara Shuzo Company
Visitors	Tel: 01463 248144
Website	www.tomatin.com
Established	1897
Status	In production
Water source	Allt na Frithe Burn
Malt source	Commercial maltsters
Phenols	Unpeated and peated (2–5 ppm)
Casks	Ex-bourbon, refill hogsheads, virgin oak and ex-sherry butts
Capacity	5 million litres of alcohol
Stills	Wash: 6 Spirit: 6
Main bottling	Legacy, NAS, 43%
Nose	Vanilla, marshmallow, pineapple and lemon.
Taste	Candy, pine, lemon sherbet, apples and sponge cake.
Finish	Light and clean.
Comments	A revamped age-statement core range is supplemented with the Cù Bòcan expressions.
Also try	Dalwhinnie, Spey Tenné, Glen Mhor
Availability	Specialist retailers, independent bottlers
Price	£27 plus

Malt	Wolfburn
Distillery	Wolfburn
	Henderson Park
	THURSO
	KW14 7XW
Owner	Aurora Brewing Ltd
Visitors	Tel: 01847 891051
Website	www.wolfburn.com
Established	2013
Status	In production
Water source	The Wolf Burn
Malt source	Commercial maltsters
Phenols	Unpeated and peated (15 ppm)
Casks	American oak quarter casks, ex-bourbon and ex-sherry
Capacity	135,000 litres litres of alcohol
Stills	Wash: 1 Spirit: 1
Main bottling	Northland, NAS, 46%
Nose	Sweet with notes of fruit and fresh sea air. Citrus with hints of cereal, and a trace of peat smoke.
Taste	Sweet, nutty tones with hints of grapes and honey in the background. Floral flavours enhanced with a hint of dried fruit and spice.
Finish	Long and refreshing.
Comments	Situated close to the old Wolfburn Distillery. Wolfburn's range is innovative and expanding.
Also try	Old Pulteney, Clynelish, Glenmorangie
Availability	Specialist retailers
Price	£40 plus

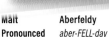

Malt	Aberfeldy
Pronounced	*aber-FELL-day*
Distillery	Aberfeldy
	ABERFELDY
	PH15 2EB
Owner	John Dewar & Sons Ltd
Visitors	Tel: 01887 822010
Website	www.aberfeldy.com
Established	1896
Status	In production
Water source	Pitilie Burn
Malt source	Commercial maltsters
Phenols	Unpeated
Casks	Refill American hogsheads and some refill European wood
Capacity	3.4 million litres of alcohol
Stills	Wash: 2 Spirit: 2
Main bottling	12 years old, 40%
Nose	Scented with spices and honeyed plump fruits.
Taste	Syrupy with lots of vanilla and fudge.
Finish	A whisper of smoke.
Comments	The bedrock malt of the Dewar's brand.
Also try	Glenmorangie, Balvenie, Glengoyne
Availability	Widespread
Price	£33 plus

Malt	Blair Athol
Pronounced	*blair-ath-ul*
Distillery	Blair Athol
	Perth Road
	PITLOCHRY
	PH16 5LY
Owner	Diageo
Visitors	Tel: 01796 482003
Website	www.malts.com
Established	1798
Status	In production
Water source	Allt Dour on Ben Vrackie
Malt source	Glen Ord Maltings
Phenols	Unpeated
Casks	Ex-bourbon refills with some ex-sherry
Capacity	2.8 million litres of alcohol
Stills	Wash: 2 Spirit: 2
Main bottling	Flora & Fauna, 12 years old, 43%
Nose	Muscat grapes and Madeira wine, brimstone in the background, even tar. Dried apricots in the foreground, and treacle toffee.
Taste	Medium- to full-bodied, but not cloying. Rich and mouth-filling, with good balance.
Finish	Sweetness at the end, after the acidity and dryish finish has passed.
Comments	Most of the production finds its way into Bell's blends. An underrated dram.
Also try	Benromach, Edradour, Longmorn
Availability	Website, specialist retailers
Price	£48 plus

Malt	**Deanston**
Distillery	Deanston
	DOUNE
	FK16 6AG
Owner	Burn Stewart Distillers Ltd
Visitors	Tel: 01786 841422
Website	www.deanstonmalt.com
Established	1965–6
Status	In production
Water source	River Teith
Malt source	Commercial maltsters
Phenols	1–2 ppm
Casks	Ex-bourbon and ex-sherry, refill ex-whisky barrels, butts and hogsheads plus de-charred, re-charred casks
Capacity	3 million litres of alcohol
Still	Wash: 2 Spirit: 2
Main bottling	12 years old, 46.3%
Nose	Fresh summer hay, malty cereal, rich creamy toffee and honeyed heather, balanced with sweet oak and barley sugar.
Taste	Smooth creamy sweetness with hints of fruit, malty honeyed spiciness and soft vanilla.
Finish	Satisfying with a tingle of cloves which lingers, then gently fades.
Comments	Relaunched dram from a distillery created from a converted cotton mill built in 1785.
Also try	The Deveron, Glenrothes, Tullibardine
Availability	Widespread
Price	£37 plus

Malt	Edradour
Pronounced	*edd-ra-DOW-er*
Distillery	Edradour
	PITLOCHRY
	PH16 5JP
Owner	The Signatory Vintage Scotch Whisky Co Ltd
Visitors	Apr-Oct, tel: 01796 472095
Website	www.edradour.com
Established	1825
Status	In production
Water source	Springs on Moulin Moor
Malt source	Bairds of Pencaitland and Inverness
Phenols	Unpeated and peated for Ballechin
Casks	Ex-bourbon and ex-sherry
Capacity	260,000 litres of alcohol
Stills	Wash: 2 Spirit: 2
Main bottling	10 years old, 40%
Nose	Peppermint, sugared almond, hint of sherry, spicy-smoky notes.
Taste	Remarkably creamy texture for a relatively light malt. Minty-clean, creamy, malty.
Finish	Mellow and warming.
Comments	Also available as peated Ballechin. A very picturesque distillery, recently expanded to double capacity.
Also try	Aberfeldy, Blair Athol, Glenturret
Availability	Specialist retailers
Price	£40 plus

Malt	**Glengoyne**
Distillery	Glengoyne
	KILLEARN
	G63 9LB
Owner	Ian Macleod Distillers Ltd
Visitors	Tel: 01360 550254
Website	www.glengoyne.com
Established	1833
Status	In production
Water source	Distillery Burn from Campsie Fells
Malt source	Simpson's, Berwick-Upon-Tweed
Phenols	Unpeated
Casks	European and American oak, ex-bourbon
Capacity	1.1 million litres of alcohol
Stills	Wash: 1 Spirit: 2
Main bottling	10 years old, 40%
Nose	Sweet, with toffee and popcorn aromas. Slightly nutty, with fresh green apples coming through.
Taste	Clean. Green apples and grass, soft oak and a hint of sweet liquorice. Water brings linseed oil and almonds.
Finish	Sweet and malty.
Comments	A fine malt from a beautifully situated distillery.
Also try	Auchentoshan, Loch Lomond, Littlemill
Availability	Everywhere
Price	£32 plus

Malt	Glenturret
Distillery	Glenturret
	The Hosh
	CRIEFF
	PH7 4HA
Owner	Lalique Group
Visitors	Tel: 01764 656565
Website	www.theglenturret.com
Established	c.1775
Status	In production
Water source	Mains water from Loch Turret
Malt source	Simpson's, Berwick-Upon-Tweed
Phenols	Unpeated and up to 80 ppm for peated expressions
Casks	Refill ex-sherry Spanish and American oak and small proportion of ex-bourbon
Capacity	500,000 litres of alcohol
Stills	Wash: 1 Spirit: 1
Sample	Triple Wood, NAS, 43%
Nose	Citrus then polished new oak, bonbons and boiled sweets with hints of cinnamon and lemon cake.
Taste	Fruity, soft and sweet. Apple and orange followed by cinnamon, toffee and wood spice. Hints of ginger and cassia with soft mellow oak
Finish	Soft, fruity and full.
Comments	The new core range also includes a sherry and a peated expression.
Also try	Blair Athol, Aberfeldy, Edradour
Availability	Specialist retailers
Price	£43 plus

Malt	Loch Lomond
Distillery	Loch Lomond
	ALEXANDRIA
	G83 0TL
Owner	Loch Lomond Group
Website	www.lochlomondwhiskies.com
Established	1966
Status	In production
Water source	Borehole aquifers and Loch Lomond
Malt source	Commercial grain dealers
Phenols	Unpeated and peated
Casks	Ex-bourbon casks
Capacity	5 million litres of alcohol
Stills	Wash: 4 Spirit: 4
Main bottling	NAS, 40%
Nose	Mellow, slightly peaty nose, with a hint of brandy butter.
Taste	Sweet cereal notes, creamy texture, pronounced brazil nuts with a citrus edge. Water brings a peppery spice with ginger and liquorice, soft malt with a honeyed structure. Distillery character of green apple and ripe pineapple melds with the cereal and honey.
Finish	Gentle, almost brulée-style finish. Light and darkly sweet with very subtle notes of orange and citrus.
Comments	The signature malt from a unique distillery which also produces single malt grain whisky. Also available as Inchmurrin.
Also try	Braeval, Glengoyne, Auchentoshan
Availability	Website, specialist retailers
Price	£25 plus

Malt	Strathearn
Distillery	Strathearn
	Bachilton Farm Steading
	METHVEN
	PH1 3QX
Owner	Douglas Laing & Co Ltd
Website	www.douglaslaing.com
Established	2013
Status	In production
Water source	Mains supply
Malt source	Commercial maltsters and locally sourced
Phenols	Unpeated and peated
Casks	European oak and ex-sherry
Capacity	30,000 litres of alcohol
Stills	Wash: 1 Spirit: 1 Gin: 1
Main bottling	5 years old, 46.6%
Nose	A dry oak style balanced by caramel with a touch of vanilla.
Taste	Sherry character with a leathery sweetness plus red fruits and cocoa.
Finish	Lingering butterscotch with honeyed barley and oat biscuits.
Comments	New ownership should bring Strathearn to a wider market.
Also try	Loch Lomond, Glenturret, Aberfeldy
Availability	Website
Price	£85

Malt	**Tullibardine**
Pronounced	*tully-BAAR-din*
Distillery	Tullibardine BLACKFORD PH4 1QG
Owner	Picard Vins & Spiritueux
Visitors	Tel: 01764 682252
Website	www.tullibardine.com
Established	1949
Status	In production
Water source	Danny Burn on Ochil Hills
Malt source	Commercial maltsters
Phenols	Unpeated
Casks	First-fill ex-bourbon and ex-sherry hogsheads and butts
Capacity	3 million litres of alcohol
Stills	Wash: 2　　Spirit: 2
Main bottling	NAS, 43%
Nose	Youthful barley with light citrus notes, a touch of candied fruit and even a hint of mint.
Taste	Initial burst of flavours of barley, lemon and vanilla. Addition of water allows these aromas to come through.
Finish	Fudge, pear drops and soft spice.
Comments	One of Bill Delmé-Evans's three distillery builds.
Also try	Deanston, Blair Athol, Aberfeldy
Availability	Specialist retailers
Price	£36 plus

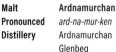

Malt	**Ardnamurchan**
Pronounced	*ard-na-mur-ken*
Distillery	Ardnamurchan
	Glenbeg
	ARDNAMURCHAN
	PH36 4JG
Owner	Adelphi Distillery Ltd
Visitors	Tel: 01972 500285
Website	www.adelphidistillery.com
Established	2014
Status	In production
Water source	Glenmore springs
Malt source	70% from Broomhall Farm and commercial maltsters
Phenols	Up to 35ppm and unpeated
Casks	Ex-bourbon and ex-sherry
Capacity	500,000 litres of alcohol
Stills	Wash: 1 Spirit: 1
Main bottling	Bottled in 2019, 57.4%
Nose	Gentle peat smoke.
Taste	Crème caramel with candied orange. Manuka honey and mango; rock salt, liquorice, maple-cured smoked bacon and extinguished peat kilns.
Finish	More smoke comes through.
Comments	Bottled as new-make spirit until 2021.
Also try	Ben Nevis, Caol Ila, Glenlochy
Availability	Distillery and specialist retailers.
Price	£55 plus

Malt	**Ben Nevis**
Distillery	Ben Nevis
	FORT WILLIAM
	PH33 6TJ
Owner	Asahi Group Holdings
Visitors	Tel: 01397 702476
Website	www.bennevisdistillery.com
Established	1825
Status	In production
Water source	Allt a'Mhuillin on Ben Nevis
Malt source	Commercial maltsters
Phenols	Up to 40ppm
Casks	Ex-bourbon and sherry
Capacity	2 million litres of alcohol
Stills	Wash: 2 Spirit: 2
Main bottling	10 years old, 46%
Nose	Sweet, malty bouquet with rich hints of smoke and vanilla.
Taste	Coats the palate firmly. Rich, full-bodied. Aromatic.
Finish	Delicious long length of finish.
Comments	Fort William's only surviving distillery.
Also try	Bowmore, GlenDronach, Scapa
Availability	Specialist retailers
Price	£50 plus

Spirit	Nc'nean
Pronounced	*nook-NEE-ann*
Distillery	Drimnin Estate
	by LOCHALINE
	PH80 6XZ
Owner	Nc'nean Distillery Ltd
Visitors	Tel: 01967 7421698
Website	www.ncnean.com
Established	2017
Status	In production
Water source	Local spring
Malt source	Certified organic from five farms, conditioned by Muntons
Phenols	Unpeated
Casks	Ex-bourbon, ex-red wine and ex-sherry
Capacity	100,000 litres of alcohol
Stills	Wash: 1 Spirit: 1
Sample	NAS, 50cl, 40%
Nose	Nutty notes of barley, a hint of salty sea breeze, camomile and herbaceous thyme.
Taste	Creamy texture with spice and pepperiness alongside grapefruit and sour berries.
Finish	Zesty and refreshing.
Comments	'Not whisky, not gin' the makers state, but 'botanical spirit' which goes well with tonic, ice and a dash of Angostura bitters. It includes wild bog myrtle, sorrel, heather and thyme and the distillate is rectified on Kintyre at Beinn an Tuirc gin distillery. The first release of malt whisky is expected in 2020.
Availability	Distillery, website and specialist retailers
Price	£30

Malt	Oban
Distillery	Oban
	OBAN
	PA34 5NH
Owner	Diageo
Visitors	Tel: 01631 572004
Website	www.malts.com
Established	1794
Status	In production
Water source	Loch Gleann a'Bhearraidh
Malt source	Roseisle Maltings
Phenols	Lightly peated
Casks Refill	American hogsheads
Capacity	870,000 litres of alcohol
Stills	Wash: 1 Spirit: 1
Main bottling	14 years old, 43%
Nose	Rich fruity sweetness, oranges, lemons and pears, with sea salt and peaty smokiness.
Taste	Full-bodied mouth-filling dried figs and honey-sweet spices followed by a smoky malty dryness.
Finish	Long, smooth and sweet with oak wood, dryness and a grain of salt.
Comments	A great place to visit when in Oban.
Also try	Ben Nevis, Bowmore, Old Pulteney
Availability	Widespread
Price	£50 plus

The Lowlands

THE growth of new distilling activity since 2000 in this area has been prolific. Once only Glenkinchie and Auchentoshan were the surviving operations but there are now 16 active malt distilleries with more on the way, including a rejuvenated Rosebank. The grain whisky-making output from the Lowlands remains the largest of any producing area. Historically, the central belt was the grain-distilling centre of Scotland as the 18th- and 19th-century Haig and Stein dynasties established and developed their businesses. Their huge Clackmannanshire distilleries produced pot-still grain spirit in vast, shallow stills that were flash-fired to distil rapidly. The result may have been commercially successful but the product was vile. The main market for it was in England where it was rectified into gin to satisfy the thirst of the masses. Robert Stein's invention of the continuous still in 1826 (see Chapter 2) ushered in a new era of whisky distilling that gained the industry its worldwide status today. Nowadays Lowland grain distilling is based at Cameron Bridge where all of Diageo's white spirit production takes place, Starlaw at Cumbernauld, North British in Edinburgh, Strathclyde in Glasgow and at Girvan in Ayrshire.

Edinburgh once boasted a large number of malt and grain distilleries but all but the venerable North British grain distillery closed. So it is heartening to see Holyrood Distillery open for business in the lee of Salisbury Crags on the city's east side. The world-famous Scotch Whisky Experience at the top of the Royal Mile (www.scotchwhiskyexperience.co.uk), just before the Castle Esplanade, continues to draw whisky enthusiasts as will the new Johnnie Walker Experience in the former House of Fraser department store on Princes Street, the focal point of Diageo's £150 million investment in Scotch whisky tourism.

The oldest distilleries in the Lowlands are Glenkinchie, Bladnoch, Auchentoshan and Rosebank while Moffat (near Airdrie), Inverleven, Kinclaith, Ladyburn, Littlemill and

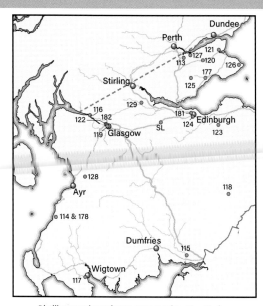

Distillery number refers to page number. SL = Starlaw

St Magdalene have gone (see page 199). The newcomers in malt production are Ailsa Bay at Girvan, Aberargie, Annandale, The Clydeside, Daftmill, Eden Mill, The Glasgow, Holyrood, InchDairnie, Lindores Abbey, Kingsbarns, Lochlea and The Borders. Burnbrae in East Kilbride is part of the Campbell Meyer blending and bottling operation and details are sparse as to its status. In the pipeline are Ardgowan, Reivers, Clutha, Crabbie's, Port of Leith, Falkirk and the as yet unnamed distillery at Moffat, Dumfriesshire.

Glenkinchie will be one of the main beneficiaries from Diageo's £150-million investment with a revamped visitor experience. Annandale's re-emergence has created an excellent facility in Dumfriesshire thanks to the deep pockets and passion for whisky of David Thomson and Teresa Church.

Stylistically Lowland malts were usually triple-distilled to create a lighter, more floral, estery and aromatic spirit. Only Auchentoshan continues with this practice which is now largely confined to Ireland. However, Rosebank when rebuilt, will be a triple-distillation operation and InchDairnie will be adopting the practice in due course.

Malt	**Aberargie**
Pronounced	*aber-AR-jee*
Distillery	Aberargie
	ABERARGIE
	PH2 9LX
Owner	The Perth Distilling Co
Established	2017
Status	In production
Water source	Private well
Malt source	Own-estate malted at Simpsons
Phenols	Unpeated
Casks	First-fill ex-sherry butts, first-fill ex-bourbon and second-fill ex-sherry and ex-bourbon casks.
Capacity	750,000 litres of alcohol
Stills	Wash: 1 Spirit: 1
Comments	No tasting samples currently available but the flavour profile will be fruity. Plans include some peated distillate. The owners bottling and blending facility is next door so only malting will be carried out offsite.

Malt	**Aerstone**
Distiller	Ailsa Bay
	GIRVAN
	KA26 9PT
Owner	William Grant & Sons Ltd
Website	www.aerstonescotchwhisky.com
Established	2007
Status	In production
Water source	Penwhapple Loch
Malt source	Commercial maltsters
Phenols	Up to 50ppm
Casks	Hudson baby ex-bourbon barrels, finished in first-fill and refill American oak.
Capacity	12 million litres of alcohol
Stills	Wash: 8 Spirit: 8
Sample	Sea Cask, 10 years old, 40%
Nose	Light and floral with a subtle, nutty character. Delicate oak, malted biscuits and creamy vanilla background.
Taste	Lightly-toasted almonds, sweet cotton candy and a gentle vanilla oak, balanced with a touch of tannin.
Finish	Lingering oak with delicate sweetness.
Comments	Part of the Girvan distilling complex. Also available as Ailsa Bay in limited volumes, output is almost wholly for blending. Ailsa Bay is micro-matured in small casks while Aerstone is also available as the Land Cask.
Also tr	Ladyburn, Caol Ila, Annandale
Availability	Specialist retailers
Price	£29 plus

Malt	Annandale
Distillery	Annandale
	Northfield
	ANNAN
	DG12 5LL
Owner	Annandale Distillery Co Ltd
Visitors	Tel: 01461 201817
Website	www.annandaledistillery.com
Established	1836. Closed 1918. Rebuilt 2014
Status	In production
Water source	Middleby Burn
Malt source	Commercial maltsters
Phenols	Up to 45ppm
Casks	Ex-bourbon and ex-sherry
Capacity	500,000 litres of alcohol
Stills	Wash: 1 Spirit: 2
Sample	Man o'Words, cask 822, 60.8%
Nose	Orangey, with barley and sultanas.
Taste	Malt, orange zest, boiled sweets and vanilla.
Finish	Some chocolate, shortbread and sweet fruit.
Comments	The distillery does not have a core range at present and bottles single cask releases under the Man o'Words (unpeated) and Man o'Sword (peated) brand names. New-make spirit is bottled as Rascally Liquor (peated and unpeated) at £25 for 50cl, 46%.
Also try	Ailsa Bay, Glasgow, Bladnoch
Availability	Website, distillery, specialist retailers
Price	£ 116 plus

Malt	**Auchentoshan**
Pronounced	*och-in-TOSH-inn*
Distillery	Auchentoshan
	DALMUIR
	G81 4SJ
Owner	Beam Suntory
Visitors	Tel: 01389 878561
Website	www.auchentoshan.com
Established	1823
Status	In production
Water source	Mains water from Loch Katrine
Malt source	Commercial maltsters
Phenols	Unpeated
Casks	Ex-bourbon barrels with some ex-sherry hogsheads and butts
Capacity	2 million litres of alcohol
Stills	Wash: 1 Intermediate: 1 Spirit: 1
Main bottling	American Oak, NAS, 40%
Nose	Bourbon-infused vanilla and coconut with layers of zesty citrus fruit.
Taste	Sweet vanilla cream, coconut and white peach.
Finish	Crisp, with sugared grapefruit and a lingering hint of spice.
Comments	The only wholly triple-distilled malt in Scotland. A fine aperitif whisky.
Also try	Bladnoch, Annandale, Glengoyne
Availability	Everywhere
Price	£25 plus

Malt	Bladnoch
Pronounced	*BLAAD-noch*
Distillery	Bladnoch
	BLADNOCH
	DG8 9AB
Owner	Bladnoch Distillery Ltd
Visitors	Tel: 01988 402605
Website	www.bladnoch.com
Established	1817
Status	In production
Water source	River Bladnoch
Malt source	Commercial maltsters
Phenols	Unpeated with occasional peated distillations
Casks	Ex-bourbon, refill hogsheads and ex-sherry butts
Capacity	1.5 million litres of alcohol
Stills	Wash: 1 Spirit: 1
Main bottling	10 years old, 46.7%
Nose	Sweet grassy notes with delicate floral aromas. Spicy oak and vanilla with hints of citrus and orange.
Taste	Spicy and sweet oak with citrus notes and hints of coconut, ginger, vanilla and gooseberry.
Finish	Clean, sweet, spicy citrus, crisp and refreshing.
Comments	A welcome return for Bladnoch under the ownership of Australian David Prior. A new café and visitor centre were opened in 2019.
Also try	Loch Lomond, Glengoyne, Arran
Availability	Distillery and specialist retailers, independent bottlers
Price	£50 plus

Malt	**The Borders**
Distillery	The Borders
	Commercial Road
	HAWICK
	TD9 7AQ
Owner	The Three Stills Co Ltd
Visitors	Tel: 01450 374330
Website	www.thebordersdistillery.com
Established	2018
Status	In production
Water source	Aquifer below the distillery
Malt source	Simpsons
Phenols	Unpeated
Casks	American and European oak
Capacity	2 million litres of alcohol
Stills	Wash: 2 Spirit: 2 Gin: 1
Comments	Tasting sample not available. Established by former employees of William Grant & Sons Ltd, The Borders will be creating malt whisky in due course. At the moment, William Kerr's Gin is the main distillate with a couple of Scotch whiskies from other sources created for retail sales.

Malt	The Clydeside
Distillery	The Clydeside
	100 Stobcross Road
	GLASGOW
	G3 8QQ
Owner	Morrison Glasgow Distillers Ltd
Visitors	Tel: 0141 212 1401
Website	www.theclydeside.com
Established	2017
Status	In production
Water source	Mains supply from Loch Katrine
Malt source	Commercial maltsters
Phenols	Unpeated
Casks	American and European oak
Capacity	500,000 litres of alcohol
Stills	Wash: 1 Spirit: 1
Comments	At the moment The Clydeside is not bottling new-make for retail sale but is selling Scotch whiskies from other sources for retail sales. The distillery tour is excellent. The flavour profile will be light but fruity.

Malt	Daftmill
Distillery	Daftmill
	by CUPAR
	KY15 5RF
Owner	Cuthbert family
Visitors	By appointment, tel: 01337 830303
Website	www.daftmill.com
Established	2005
Status	In production
Water source	Artesian well on the farm
Malt source	Own-estate, conditioned by Crisp Malt of Alloa
Phenols	Unpeated
Casks	Ex-bourbon and ex-sherry
Capacity	90–100,000 litres of alcohol
Stills	Wash: 1 Spirit: 1
Sample	2019 Summer Batch Release, 2008, 46%
Nose	Deep vanilla aroma reminiscent of crème brulée with some tinned peaches, dried cocoa powder and a delicate grassy note.
Taste	Fresh fruit explodes on the palate with green apples, pears and some melon, developing into soft peach and a slight tropical note. Herbaceous almost earthy note on the mid-palate.
Finish	Oak appears again, offering vanilla pods, clove, cinnamon and some melted honey.
Comments	At last Daftmill has come to market. The early promise has been fulfilled.
Also try	Loch Lomond, Glengoyne, Arran
Availability	Berry Brothers & Rudd and specialist retailers
Price	Seasonal releases are sold via ballot by BB&R. £93 plus

Malt	Eden Mill
Distillery	Eden Mill
	Main Street
	GUARDBRIDGE
	KY16 0UU
Owner	St Andrews Brewers Ltd
Visitors	By appointment, tel: 01334 834038
Website	www.edenmill.com
Established	2014
Status	In production
Water source	Not known
Malt source	Simpsons
Phenols	Not known
Casks	Ex-bourbon and ex-sherry
Capacity	100,000 litres of alcohol
Stills	Wash: 1 Spirit: 1 Gin: 1
Sample	2019 Release, 46.5%
Nose	Sherry-forward aromas. Reminiscent of cherry sweetness, notes of vanilla fudge with hints of spiciness throughout. Light hint of spice.
Taste	Light, sweet spice notes of toasted fruits. Remains sweet with hints of cocoa and caramel. Malty-sweet at the end.
Finish	Biscuit sweetness and sherry flavours fade to a spicy peppery character, which in turn develops with an aromatic cassia spice.
Comments	Known primarily for its large range of gins, Eden Mill is now creating its first malt whisky
Also try	Loch Lomond, Daftmill, Strathearn
Availability	Website, distillery and specialist retailers
Price	£79

Malt	The Glasgow
Distillery	Glasgow
	Hillington
	GLASGOW
	G52 4XB
Owner	Glasgow Distillery Co Ltd
Visitors	By appointment, tel: 0141 404 7191
Website	www.glasgowdistillery.com
Established	2014
Status	In production
Water source	Mains supply
Malt source	Commercial maltsters
Phenols	Peated up to 50ppm and unpeated
Casks	Ex-bourbon, ex-sherry and virgin oak
Capacity	500,000 litres of alcohol
Stills	Wash: 2 Spirit: 2 Gin: 1
Main bottling	2019 Release, 50cl, 46%
Nose	Dried dark fruits with tropical undertones, hints of biscuit, oak and freshly cut grass.
Taste	Sweet butterscotch with crème brulée. Hints of freshly sliced pear, dried figs, dates and raisin with sweet almond, honey and creamy shortbread notes.
Finish	Long. Freshly spread marmalade, nutmeg notes underpinned by complex woodiness and a slight spice.
Comments	Glasgow is an expanding, innovative distillery with interesting, award-winning spirits including a peated malt with a triple-distilled expression due soon.
Also try	Loch Lomond, Daftmill, Bladnoch
Availability	Website and specialist retailers
Price	£49

Malt	Glenkinchie
Pronounced	*glen-KIN-chee*
Distillery	Glenkinchie PENCAITLAND EH34 5ET
Owner	Diageo
Visitors	Tel: 01875 342004
Website	www.malts.com
Established	1837
Status	In production
Water source	Local spring
Malt source	Roseisle Maltings
Phenols	Lightly peated
Casks	Ex-bourbon casks
Capacity	2.5 million litres of alcohol
Stills	Wash: 1 Spirit: 1
Main bottling	12 years old, 43%
Nose	Aromatic, vanilla, cut flowers and beneath, a clean, toasty note. Fresh citrus, lemon cheesecake.
Taste	Light, smooth-bodied. Sweet, becoming flowery, then butter icing, lemon cheesecake and freesias.
Finish	Herbal and drying, a little like pot-pourri.
Comments	Diageo is investing heavily in the visitor facilities at its premier Lowland distillery.
Also try	Bladnoch, Glen Moray, Auchentoshan
Availability	Widespread
Price	£40 plus

Malt	Holyrood
Pronounced	*holy-rood*
Distillery	Holyrood
	St Leonard's Lane
	EDINBURGH
	EH8 9SH
Owner	The Holyrood Distillery Ltd
Visitors	Tel: 0131 285 8973
Website	www.holyrooddistillery.co.uk
Established	2019
Status	In production
Water source	Mains supply
Malt source	Crisp maltings
Phenols	Peated (55ppm) and unpeated
Casks	Mostly ex-bourbon, ex-sherry, ex-port
Capacity	350,000 litres of alcohol
Stills	Wash: 1 Spirit: 1 Gin: 1
Comments	Edinburgh's most recently established distillery will be producing malt whisky but as yet is relying on its gin range to raise revenue. The visitor facilities are excellent.

Malt	InchDairnie
Pronounced	*inch-DAIR-nay*
Distillery	InchDairnie
	Whitecraig's Road
	GLENROTHES
	KY6 2RX
Owner	John Fergus & Co Ltd
Website	www.inchdairniedistillery.com
Established	2016
Status	In production
Water source	Mains supply
Malt source	Muntons and Boortmalt, all Fife-grown
Phenols	Peated (20ppm for Kinglassie) and unpeated
Casks	Ex-bourbon and ex-wine hogsheads, ex-Andalusian fortified wine
Capacity	2 million litres of alcohol
Stills	Wash: 1 Lomond: 1 Spirit: 1
Comments	The spirit character is grassy, flowery and fruity with notes of vanilla and wine from the wood. Still a work in progress. Under Ian Palmer's direction InchDairnie's output will be flavour-driven with a rye expression (RyeLaw) to the fore. Expect the single malt around 2029.

Malt	**Kingsbarns**
Distillery	Kingsbarns
	East Newhall Farm
	ST ANDREWS
	KY16 8QE
Owner	The Kingsbarns Company of Distillers Ltd
Visitors	Tel: 01333 451300
Website	www.kingsbarnsdistillery.com
Established	2014
Status	In production
Water source	Borehole aquifer
Malt source	Fife-grown barley conditioned at Muntons
Phenols	Unpeated
Casks	First-fill ex-bourbon and reconditioned ex-wine barriques
Capacity	600,000 litres of alcohol
Stills	Wash: 1 Spirit: 1 Gin: 1
Main bottling	Dream to Dram, NAS, 46%
Nose	Banana, pineapple syrup and summer berries, with a slight herbal note.
Taste	Fruity, floral and balanced, soft toffee, custard pastry and redcurrants.
Finish	Ginger syrup.
Comments	The Wemyss family have ensured that Kingsbarns will prosper.
Also try	Daftmill, Bladnoch, Annandale
Availability	Distillery and specialist retailers.
Price	£45 plus

Malt	Lindores
Pronounced	*linn-DOORS*
Distillery	Lindores Abbey
	Abbey Road
	NEWBURGH
	KY14 6HH
Owner	The Lindores Distilling Co Ltd
Visitors	Tel: 01337 842547
Website	www.lindoresabbeydistillery.com
Established	2017
Status	In production
Water source	Borehole aquifer
Malt source	Own-estate barley conditioned at Muntons
Phenols	0.5ppm
Casks	Ex-bourbon, ex-sherry and STRs
Capacity	250,000 litres of alcohol
Stills	Wash: 1 Spirit: 2
Sample	Aqua Vitae, NAS, 40%
Nose	Peaches and pears.
Taste	Citrus with cinnamon, cloves and ginger.
Finish	Zesty with caramel and herbal notes.
Comments	This distillery can claim to be the spiritual home of whisky as records from 1494 mention *aqua vitae*. 2020 will see the first release of its malt whisky. Aqua Vitae is distilled using locally grown green herbs and spices.
Availability	Distillery and specialist retailers.
Price	£40

Malt	Lochlea
Distiller	Lochlea
	Lochlea Farm, Craigie
	KILMARNOCK
	KA1 5NN
Owner	Lochlea Distilling Co Ltd
Visitors	Tel: 01292 541222
Established	2018
Status	In production
Water source	Borehole aquifer
Malt source	Own-estate barley conditioned at Bairds
Phenols	Unpeated
Casks	First- and second-fill ex-bourbon barrels, ex-Oloroso and PX sherry butts, STRs, some ex-Port, rum and red wine casks, heavily peated refill quarter casks and barrels
Capacity	360,000 litres of alcohol
Stills	Wash: 1 Spirit: 1
Sample	New Make, 63.5%
Nose	Estery, tropical fruit, citrus and slightly floral.
Taste	Orchard fruits, touch of citrus
Finish	Extremely smooth.
Comments	Not available at present but another Lowland to welcome. Malcolm Rennie has been in charge of production. The distillery is situated on one of the farms where Robert Burns lived during his short life.

Malt	Rosebank
Distillery	Rosebank
	Camelon
	FALKIRK
	FK1 5JR
Owner	Ian Macleod Distillers Ltd
Website	www.rosebank.com
Established	c.1840. Closed 1993.
Status	Under reconstruction in 2020
Water source	Loch Carron
Malt source	Simpsons
Phenols	Unpeated
Casks	Mostly ex-bourbon, some first-refill casks and others for experimentation
Capacity	1 million litres of alcohol
Stills	Wash: 1 Spirit: 1 Intermediate: 1
Sample	433, distilled in 1993, 53.3%
Nose	Hints of vanilla, mango, raspberry, barley sugar and lavender.
Taste	Silky and light with complex flavours of cranachan, lemon, floral notes, marzipan and faint spice.
Finish	Citrus with hints of ripe fruit and oak.
Comments	Distillery now under reconstruction. Bottlings are currently rare and very expensive.
Also try	Auchentoshan, Glengoyne, Glenkinchie
Availability	Website, specialist retailers and independent bottlers.
Price	£1,150 plus

Islay

ISLAY malt whisky is perhaps the most characteristic category of all. However, the island's product – traditionally the heaviest and most pungent available – does conceal a few surprises. The Islay style is due to production methods which were developed in concert with the available distilling ingredients in this remote locality. Renowned as the most fertile island in the Hebrides, Islay had three major assets in this regard: a ready source of local bere or barley, inexhaustible amounts of peat and burns running brimful with soft water. Coupled to this was the likelihood that the art of distilling was probably brought to Islay from Ireland by the MacBeatha clan, hereditary physicians to the MacDonalds, the Lords of the Isles until 1493, who gifted them land in the Kilchoman area.

While the urban markets were supplied by mainland distillers in the 18th and 19th centuries, the islanders supplied local markets from stills – both legal and illegal – which were operated from farmyards, bothies in the remote glens above Port Ellen and caves along the precipitous coast of the Oa.

It is impossible to visit Islay and not notice the peat. Crossing the enormous Laggan Moss between Port Ellen and Bowmore the peat banks stretch as far as the eye can see. This fuel was the only means by which the islanders could dry their grain – an essential process not only in distilling, but also for storage during the wet season. By kilning barley it could be kept for longer and the drier the grain was, the less likely it was to go mouldy.

As the grain dried in the peat smoke, it imparted a highly distinctive character which manifested itself when the spirit was finally distilled from it. These flavours are still apparent in most of today's Islay malts and are best experienced by trying Ardbeg, Lagavulin, Laphroaig, Port Ellen, Kilchoman and Octomore (from Bruichladdich). The latter pair are more recent malts being produced in the traditional Islay style while the first four are all from the Kildalton parish along Islay's

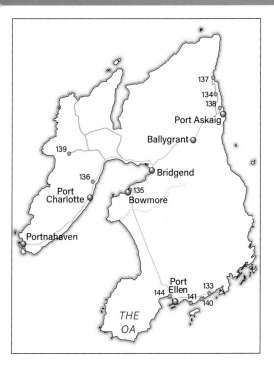

Distillery number refers to page number

southern coast. The other Islays of Bruichladdich, Bunna-habhain and Caol Ila display the peaty-smoky accent to a far lesser degree depending on the expression. For those new to the world of malt Bunnahabhain is an excellent entrée to the Islays and is a fine aperitif malt. The latest addition to the Islay stable is Ardnahoe on the Sound of Islay and another distillery is at the planning stages, to be situated near Port Ellen and provisionally named Farkin, financed by Elixir Distillers of London. Gartbreck Distillery near Bowmore is still in gestation as land ownership issues and other factors have stalled its construction. Watch this space, as they say. But there must be a point when the Islay brand becomes diluted if many more distilleries are allowed. Perhaps this point has been reached already?

Anyone who does venture over to this beautiful island will be struck by the fact that all the Islay distilleries are in coastal locations. The reason? During the mid-to-late 19th century the sea was the 'road' to the mainland markets and all the distilleries were directly accessible by boat so commerce and the provision of supplies such as coal and casks were better facilitated. In contrast the smaller inland farm distilleries fell victim to their more remote locations and gradually closed down. Remnants of some of these are still visible at Octomore above Port Charlotte, Tallant Farm above Bowmore and Lossit Kennels near Bridgend. The surviving distilleries all cater for visitors to Islay and there is a particularly good café at Ardbeg.

Port Ellen Distillery is being resurrected by Diageo and will benefit from the same investment that will see Caol Ila's visitor facilities ramped up to a new level. Behind all this new activity, Port Ellen Maltings continue to supply most of the malt requirements for the island's distilleries.

For those wishing to submerge themselves in the whole Islay experience the Islay Whisky Academy (www.islaywhiskyacademy.scot) runs educational residential courses.

The Islays in general should be approached with great respect since they are that part of the master blender's palette which he uses sparingly to help create the blends which have been the bedrock of the industry for over 150 years.

Malt	Ardbeg
Pronounced	*aard-BEGG*
Distillery	Ardbeg
	PORT ELLEN
	PA42 7EB
Owner	LVMH
Visitors	Tel: 01496 302244
Website	www.ardbeg.com
Established	1815
Status	In production
Water source	Loch Uigeadail
Malt source	Port Ellen Maltings
Phenols	55–65 ppm
Casks	First and second refill ex-bourbon with some ex-sherry
Capacity	2.4 million litres of alcohol
Stills	Wash: 2 Spirit: 2
Main bottling	10 years old, 46%
Nose	Intense smoky fruit and effervescent peat.
Taste	Tangy lemon and lime and warm creamy cappuccino.
Finish	Long, smoky, aniseedy and almondy.
Comments	A sublime Islay, right up the peat scale.
Also try	Lagavulin, Ledag, Port Ellen
Availability	Everywhere
Price	£40 plus

Malt	Ardnahoe
Distillery	Ardnahoe
	PORT ASKAIG
	PA46 7RU
Owner	Hunter Laing & Co Ltd
Visitors	Tel: 01496 840711
Website	www.ardnahoedistillery.com
Established	2018
Status	In production
Water source	Loch Ardnahoe
Malt source	Port Ellen Maltings
Phenols	5–40ppm
Casks	First-fill ex-bourbon and ex-oloroso
Capacity	1 million litres of alcohol
Stills	Wash: 1 Spirit: 1
Comments	The flavour profile will be the classically peated Islay style: smoky, dynamic and full-bodied. Islay's newest distillery (there could be more!) is situated in a stunning location offering a great visitor experience. Jim McEwan (ex-Bowmore and Bruichladdich) commissioned production.

Malt	**Bowmore**
Pronounced	*bow-MORE*
Distillery	Bowmore
	School Street
	BOWMORE
	PA43 7GS
Owner	Beam Suntory
Visitors	Tel: 01496 810441
Website	www.bowmore.com
Established	1779
Status	In production
Water source	River Laggan
Malt source	Floor maltings 30% and Simpsons
Phenols	25–30ppm
Casks	Ex-bourbon barrels, hogsheads and ex-sherry butts
Capacity	2 million litres of alcohol
Stills	Wash: 2 Spirit: 2
Main bottling	12 years old, 40%
Nose	Subtle notes of lemon and honey bound in a distinctive smokiness.
Taste	Medium-bodied, warming mouthfeel revealing exotic fruits, subtle dark chocolate and peat smoke.
Finish	Lingering peat smoke.
Comments	An Islay stalwart, perennially popular.
Also try	Glen Scotia, Springbank, Highland Park
Availability	Everywhere
Price	£30 plus

Malt	Bruichladdich
Pronounced	*broo-ick-LADD-ay*
Distillery	Bruichladdich
	BRUICHLADDICH
	PA49 7UN
Owner	Rémy Cointreau
Visitors	Tel: 01496 850190
Website	www.bruichladdich.com
Established	1881
Status	In production
Water source	Bruichladdich Burn
Malt source	50% local (of which 5% organic) and Bairds
Phenols	Unpeated
Casks	First-fill ex-bourbon, ex-wine and ex-sherry finishes
Capacity	1.5 million litres of alcohol
Stills	Wash: 2 Spirit: 2
Main bottling	The Classic Laddie, NAS, 50%
Nose	Barley sugar and a hint of mint, freshly cut wild flowers – buttercup, daisy, meadowsweet, myrtle, primrose and cherry blossom. With a dash of water, lemon drops and honey, tangerine and tablet.
Taste	Sweet oak and barley, ripe green fruit, brown sugar and sweet malt.
Finish	Zesty and refreshing.
Comments	The installation of Saladin Box maltings will complete the entire production process on Islay. The Botanist gin is made here.
Also try	Jura, Bunnahabhain, Springbank
Availability	Everywhere
Price	£40 plus

Malt	**Bunnahabhain**
Pronounced	*bonna-HAAV-inn*
Distillery	Bunnahabhain
	PORT ASKAIG
	PA46 7RP
Owner	Burn Stewart Distillers Ltd
Visitors	Tel: 01496 840646
Website	www.bunnahabhain.com
Established	1881
Status	In production
Water source	Margadale Spring
Malt source	Unpeated from Simpsons, peated malt from Port Ellen Maltings
Phenols	35–40ppm
Casks	Fresh ex-bourbon and ex-sherry with various ex-wine, port, marsala and wine casks
Capacity	3.2 million litres of alcohol
Stills	Wash: 2 Spirit: 2
Main bottling	12 years old, 46.3%
Nose	Fresh and aromatic, fruity floral with hints of dried fruit and a subtle prevalence of smoke.
Taste	Light with fruit notes, nutty flavours with a sweetness and slight hints of vanilla and caramel.
Finish	Lingering, beautifully rich and full-bodied.
Comments	A revamped range from a distillery that is undergoing a huge renovation.
Also try	Bruichladdich, Tobermory, Loch Lomond
Availability	Widespread
Price	£40 plus

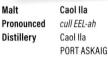

Malt	Caol Ila
Pronounced	*cull EEL-ah*
Distillery	Caol Ila
	PORT ASKAIG
	PA46 7RL
Owner	Diageo
Visitors	Tel: 01496 302760
Website	www.malts.com
Established	1846
Status	In production
Water source	Loch Nam Ban
Malt source	Port Ellen Maltings
Phenols	Unpeated and up to 35 ppm
Casks	Refill American oak hogsheads, European oak butts
Capacity	6.5 million litres of alcohol
Stills	Wash: 3 Spirit: 3
Main bottling	12 years old, 43%
Nose	Fresh and appetising. Subdued, citric fruitiness: a whiff of bath oil and dentist's mouthwash with little or no trace of smoke.
Taste	Smooth, pleasant mouth-feel: firm with a light to medium body. Drinks well at natural strength: sweet start; pleasant, light fragrant smokiness.
Finish	Lengthy, sweet smokiness, slightly sour.
Comments	New investment will make Caol Ila a major visitor attraction.
Also try	Talisker, Ledaig, Kilchoman
Availability	Widespread
Price	£43 plus

Malt	Kilchoman
Pronounced	*kill-HOM-ann*
Distillery	Kilchoman
	Rockside Farm
	BRUICHLADDICH
	PA49 7UT
Owner	Kilchoman Distillery Co Ltd
Visitors	Tel: 01496 850011
Website	www.kilchomandistillery.com
Established	2005
Status	In production
Water source	Allt Glean Osmail
Malt source	Floor maltings 30% and Port Ellen Maltings
Phenols	Up to 50ppm
Casks	Ex-bourbon, ex-sherry and ex-red wine, STR
Capacity	480,000 litres of alcohol
Stills	Wash: 2 Spirit: 2
Main bottling	Machir Bay, NAS, 46%
Nose	Lemon zest, vanilla and distinct coastal influence give way to floral intensity, juicy peaches, pears, and wafts of rich spices.
Taste	Bursts of tropical fruit and dried sultanas, warming smoke and waves of honey, malt, butterscotch and rich sweetness.
Finish	Sherry-soaked fruit, cracked black pepper and sea salt. Long-lasting with layers of citrus sweetness and maritime peat smoke.
Comments	Kilchoman has been newly expanded.
Also try	Ailsa Bay, Ardbeg, Port Charlotte
Availability	Website, distillery, specialist retailers
Price	£43 plus

Malt	**Lagavulin**
Pronounced	*laga-VOOL-inn*
Distillery	Lagavulin PORT ELLEN PA42 7DX
Owner	Diageo
Visitors	Tel: 01496 302749
Website	www.malts.com
Established	1816
Status	In production
Water source	Solum Lochs
Malt source	Port Ellen Maltings
Phenols	30–35 ppm
Casks	Refill American hogsheads, refill European wood, ex-sherry
Capacity	2.53 million litres of alcohol
Stills	Wash: 2 Spirit: 2
Main bottling	16 years old, 43%
Nose	Intensely flavoured, peat smoke with iodine and seaweed and a rich, deep sweetness.
Taste	Full-bodied. Rich. Dry peat smoke fills the palate with sweetness, followed by sea and salt with touches of wood.
Finish	A long, elegant peat-filled finish with lots of salt and seaweed.
Comments	A flagship malt from Diageo.
Also try	Ardbeg, Annandale, Ailsa Bay
Availability	Everywhere
Price	£50 plus

Malt	Laphroaig
Pronounced	*la-froyg*
Distillery	Laphroaig
	PORT ELLEN
	PA42 7DU
Owner	Beam Suntory
Visitors	Tel: 01496 302496
Website	www.laphroaig.com
Established	1815
Status	In production
Water source	Kilbride Dam, Loch na Beinn Breac
Malt source	Floor maltings 30% and Port Ellen Maltings
Phenols	3–40 ppm
Casks	Ex-bourbon, new European oak, ex-sherry and quarter casks
Capacity	3.3 million litres of alcohol
Stills	Wash: 3 Spirit: 4
Main bottling	10 years old, 40%
Nose	Medicinal, well-balanced, peaty-smoky. Delightfully pungent. A hospital corridor?
Taste	Big, peaty flavour. Surprisingly sweet and salty.
Finish	Long, lingering with the sweetness dying slowly.
Comments	A legendary Islay malt
Also try	Lagavulin, Port Ellen, Brora
Availability	Everywhere
Price	£35 plus

Malt	**Octomore**
Pronounced	*okto-MORE*
Distillery	Bruichladdich
	BRUICHLADDICH
	PA49 7UN
Owner	Rémy Cointreau
Visitors	Tel: 01496 850190
Website	www.bruichladdich.com
Established	1881
Status	In production
Water source	Bruichladdich Burn
Malt source	50% local (of which 5% organic) and Bairds
Phenols	Up to 208ppm
Casks	First-fill American oak casks
Capacity	1.5 million litres of alcohol
Stills	Wash: 2 Spirit: 2 Gin: 1
Sample	Release 10.1, 5 years old, 59.8%, 107ppm
Nose	Vanilla-led, caramel, hints of smoke, candied apple, gooseberry and marzipan.
Taste	Soft yet powerful and warming, peppery, barley sugar, smoky – dried earth and hints of rubber. Warm sand, sweetness of charred oak and pineapple.
Finish	Sweetness from tablet/fudge and a mix of peat smoke and cold marine air.
Comments	The world's most peated malt whisky in a very complex range of expressions.
Also try	Ailsa Bay, Ardbeg, Lagavulin
Availability	Website, distillery, specialist retailers
Price	£125 plus

Malt	Port Charlotte
Distillery	Bruichladdich
	BRUICHLADDICH
	PA49 7UN
Owner	Rémy Cointreau
Visitors	Tel: 01496 850190
Website	www.bruichladdich.com
Established	1881
Status	In production
Water source	Bruichladdich Burn
Malt source	50% local (of which 5% organic) and Bairds
Phenols	40ppm
Casks	First-fill American oak casks
Capacity	1.5 million litres of alcohol
Stills	Wash: 2 Spirit: 2
Sample	PC 10 years old, 50%
Nose	Maritime, smoke, dry, earthy, golden caramel, fudge, vanilla custard, hints of ginger, nutmeg and clove.
Taste	Coconut, vanilla custard, lemon honey combine with smoked oysters and sun-baked salty sand.
Finish	Smoke, sweet fudge, orange, mango and banoffee pie.
Comments	The mid-range peated malt from Bruichladdich.
Also try	Bowmore, Ledaig, Lagavulin
Availability	Website, distillery, specialist retailers
Price	£50 plus

Malt	Port Ellen
Distillery	Port Ellen
	PORT ELLEN
	PA42 7AF
Owner	Diageo
Website	www.malts.com
Established	1825. Closed 1983.
Status	Under reconstruction in 2020
Water source	Leorin Lochs
Malt source	Port Ellen Maltings
Phenols	Not known
Casks	Not known
Capacity	1 million litres of alcohol
Sample	Untold Stories, 37 years old, 1979, 17th Release, 51%
Nose	Light yet complex. Peat-reek, damp bark, charred wax, flowers and tropical fruits, then chamois leather and sherbet lemon. Scented wood smoke.
Taste	Smooth, oily, sweet and fruity. Lemony citrus with fragrant damp grass and spicy smoked meats. Freshly sliced apple liven things up.
Finish	Smooth, warming and spicy, with aromatic smoke.
Comments	Extremely rare and the new distillery won't increase that supply for several years.
Also try	Ardbeg, Brora, Port Charlotte
Availability	Website and specialist retailers
Price	£1,500 plus

Campbeltown

CAMPBELTOWN was the Victorian capital of distilling in Scotland with 20 active distilleries when the advertising agent turned whisky writer Alfred Barnard visited in 1886 on his grand tour of the distilleries of the United Kingdom. At that time the portfolio was Albyn (1830), Ardlussa (1879), Argyll (1844), Benmore (1868), Burnside (1825), Campbeltown (1815), Dalaruan (1824), Dalintober (1832), Glen Nevis (1877), Glengyle (1872) Glenside (1830), Kinloch (1823), Kintyre (c.1826), Lochhead (1824), Lochruan (1835), Longrow (1824), Rieclachan (1825), Scotia (1832), Springbank (1828) and Springside (1830).

These operations were a throwback to the days when illicit distilling in the surrounding district was rife; between 1797 and 1817 no legal whisky was distilled in this area but after the Excise Act of 1823, distilling in the region largely went legal with 13 distilleries being established within a decade of the new legislation. For the next century or so, Campbeltown boomed and the town prospered until the industry eventually collapsed in the 1920s. The reasons? Primarily demand dropped for Campbeltown whisky as the blenders gravitated towards Speyside and Islay for their component malts. There was a great deal of over-production as well, and many distillery closures were followed by years of trustees and liquidators trying to sell off stock that few wanted. Only Springbank and Glen Scotia survived this disastrous period until rejoined by a resurgent Glengyle in 2004.

It would be unwise, however, to forget Campbeltown's contribution to distilling in Scotland. It remains one of the five official SWA appellations and its malts had a distinctive character which, in their heyday, resembled that of Islay. Modern-day Springbank is a very elegant whisky which is distilled two-and-half times in a complex arrangement of charging one wash still and two spirit stills. This distillery is unique on many fronts. It is the only distillery to malt all its own barley (and Glengyle's), it bottles its own products, it is still in family hands and it produces another two malts, Hazelburn and Longrow, of differing character character. Today, Longrow perhaps comes closest to the old Campbeltown style. Springbank's survival is a tribute to the quality of its three malt whiskies.

Despite its relative remoteness at the heel of Kintyre, the trip to Campbeltown can be undertaken as part of a tour to Islay and there is plenty of accommodation in the town which has seen a lot of investment in local tourism recently. The Campbeltown Malts Festival in May showcases the best whiskies the town produces and a number of other themed festivals keeps the summer season ticking over. The Ardshiel Hotel hosts a Friday Dram Club and it's good to see the suggestion I made in the last edition for a walking tour of the town's old distilling heritage has come to fruition under Glen Scotia's initiative.

While Campbeltown no longer has the status it once had it is still an absolutely essential destination for any whisky lover on their journey through the Scotch whisky landscape.

Malt	Glen Scotia
Pronounced	*glen SKOASH-ah*
Distillery	Glen Scotia
	High Street
	CAMPBELTOWN
	PA28 6DS
Owner	Loch Lomond Group
Visitors	Tel: 01586 552288
Website	www.glenscotia.com
Established	1832
Status	In production
Water source	Crosshill Loch and borehole aquifers
Malt source	Commercial maltsters
Phenols	Unpeated and peated, up to 55ppm
Casks	First-fill ex-bourbon and ex-sherry
Capacity	800,000 litres of alcohol
Stills	Wash: 1 Spirit: 1
Main bottling	Double Cask, NAS, 40%
Nose	Crème caramel, caramelised fruit sugars, wood sugar, toffee and fudge before some apple and peach come through. In time a charred note of bourbon with a pleasing dusty dryness. Has some power.
Taste	Sweet, tongue-tingling, good mid-palate weight, dry with good depth. A dash of water adds some dried mint.
Finish	Deep and dark.
Comments	The revamped range of expressions is a welcome addition to the Campbeltown whiskyscape.
Also try	Springbank, Oban, Jura
Availability	Specialist retailers
Price	£35 plus

Malt	Hazelburn
Distillery	Springbank
	CAMPBELTOWN
	PA28 6ET
Owner	J&A Mitchell & Co Ltd
Website	www.springbank.scot
Established	1828
Status	In production
Water source	Crosshill Loch
Malt source	Floor maltings
Phenols	Unpeated
Casks	Ex-bourbon, ex-sherry and refill hogsheads
Capacity	750,000 litres of alcohol
Stills	Wash: 1 Spirit: 2
Main bottling	10 years old, 46%
Nose	Stewed pears and baked apples are followed by honeycomb and fudge notes.
Taste	Rich with vanilla and honey flavours, liquorice follows with a refreshing zestiness.
Finish	A refined milk-chocolate cream finish that is oily and chewy.
Comments	Triple-distilled and the lightest of the Springbank whiskies.
Also try	Auchentoshan, Rosebank, Glen Scotia
Availability	Specialist retailers
Price	£38 plus

Malt	Kilkerran
Distillery	Glengyle
	Glengyle Road
	CAMPBELTOWN
	PA28 6EX
Owner	J&A Mitchell & Co Ltd
Website	www.kilkerran.scot
Established	1872. Closed 1925–2004.
Status	In production
Water source	Crosshill Loch
Malt source	Springbank Distillery floor maltings
Phenols	8-10 ppm and 84ppm
Casks	Ex-bourbon, ex-sherry and refill hogsheads
Capacity	750,000 litres of alcohol
Stills	Wash: 1 Spirit: 1
Main bottling	12 years old, 46%
Nose	Dominant oak notes, toasted marshmallows, dried fruit pudding, cherries, marzipan and a hint of peat.
Taste	Fruity with citrus notes and orange peel, then vanilla, butterscotch, honeycomb and digestive biscuits.
Finish	Velvety smooth with lemon meringue and that classic Campbeltown salty oiliness.
Comments	Now also bottling an 8-year-old cask strength and a heavily peated expression.
Also try	Oban, Glen Scotia, Clynelish
Availability	Specialist retailers
Price	£37 plus

Malt	**Longrow**
Distillery	Springbank
	Longrow
	CAMPBELTOWN
	PA28 6ET
Owner	J&A Mitchell & Co Ltd
Website	www.springbank.scot
Established	1828
Status	In production
Water source	Crosshill Loch
Malt source	Floor maltings
Phenols	50–55ppm
Casks	Ex-bourbon, ex-sherry and refill hogsheads
Capacity	750,000 litres of alcohol
Stills	Wash: 1 Spirlt: 2
Main bottling	Peated, NAS, 46%
Nose	Very creamy, vanilla custard. The smoke develops and toasted marshmallows, herbs and rich fruits appear over time.
Taste	Well balanced – rich and creamy with a medicinal hint. The smoke is always present and washes over the palate in waves.
Finish	Sweet peat smoke lingers long, mouthfilling, moreish.
Comments	A double-distilled classic throwback to the old-fashioned Campbeltown style.
Also try	Caol Ila, Brora, Ardmore
Availability	Specialist retailers
Price	£40 plus

Malt	Springbank
Distillery	Springbank
	Longrow
	CAMPBELTOWN
	PA28 6ET
Owner	J&A Mitchell & Co Ltd
Visitors	Tel: 01586 552009
Website	www.springbank.scot
Established	1828
Status	In production
Water source	Crosshill Loch
Malt source	Floor maltings
Phenols	12–15ppm
Casks	Ex-bourbon, ex-sherry and refill hogsheads
Capacity	750,000 litres of alcohol
Stills	Wash: 1 Spirit: 2
Main bottling	10 years old, 46%
Nose	Orchard pears with a hint of peat, vanilla and malt.
Taste	Malt, oak, spice, nutmeg and cinnamon, vanilla essence.
Finish	Sweet with a lingering salty tingle.
Comments	Two-and-half-times distilled. A class act from Campbeltown that gets better the longer it matures.
Also try	Kilkerran, Glen Scotia, Bunnahabhain
Availability	Widespread
Price	£42

Islands

THIS region, which the SWA insists is a Highland producing region, is anything but, extending from Orkney in the north to Arran in the south (whisky, as yet, is not distilled on Shetland). Wallace and I always felt it should stand alone and perhaps one day the SWA will change that.

The total number of Island distilleries currently active is 11, an increase of four since 2010. The new operations are Abhainn Dearg on Harris (2008) which has been joined by Harris Distillery on the same Outer Hebridean island (2015). On Skye Torabhaig has been created on Sleat to accompany the world-famous Talisker. On the neighbouring Isle of Raasay, the distillery of the same name was built in 2017 while to the south of the region, Lagg Distillery, sister to Arran Distillery, started in 2019. There are ongoing plans for distilleries on Barra and the Uists, but they are in the early stages.

Arran Distillery at Lochranza was the last new operation to be built in the 20th century and celebrated its 21st anniversary in 2016. Lagg is planned to take over production of Machrie Moor, the peated expression of Isle of Arran malt.

Diageo's Talisker continues its position as one of the most successful award-winning single malts with a plethora of NAS bottlings which some consumers might find confusing. If in doubt go for the main trade bottling at 10 years old and 57.8% abv, the strength at which all the distillery's expressions are bottled.

Highland Park remains a perennial favourite but again the number of NAS expressions can seem a bit daunting. Neighbouring Scapa is good value. Tobermory's peated expression, Ledaig, is making ground and is well-presented. Similarly Jura has a full stable of NAS bottlings but Tobermory remains faithful to the age statement (as does Ledaig).

The heritage of distilling in the islands is well recorded and was something on which the island clan chiefs placed great value. However, heavy drinking and the subsequent social problems it created was a big problem in the clan society

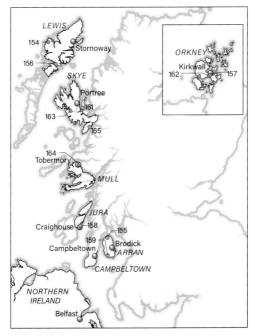

Distillery number refers to page number.

of the Hebrides and in 1609 the import of strong wines and aquavitae was banned while home-brewing and distillation for private use was allowed to continue. That craft was the bedrock from which the industry evolved out of the crofts and farmyards and into the multi-million pound businesses that now exist throughout the islands.

The Island malt whisky styles are variable and display distillery characteristics from the heather-honey signature of Highland Park to the maritime pepper finish of Talisker. Along the way you will discover Jura's Highland flavour, Tobermory's light peatiness and Arran's floral freshness. We'll have to wait a while to savour aged expressions of Harris, Lagg, Raasay and Torabhaig, but it will be worth it.

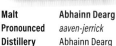

Malt	**Abhainn Dearg**
Pronounced	*aaven-jerrick*
Distillery	Abhainn Dearg
	Carnish
	ISLE OF LEWIS
	HS2 9EX
Owner	Mark Tayburn
Visitors	Tel: 01851 672429
Website	www.abhainndearg.co.uk
Established	2008
Status	In production
Water source	Abhainn Dearg (Red River)
Malt source	Locally grown and malted
Phenols	Peated (up to 40ppm) and unpeated
Casks	Ex-bourbon and ex-Oloroso, Madeira and ex-red and white wine, virgin oak
Capacity	25,000 litres of alcohol
Stills	Wash: 1 Spirit: 2
Sample	3 years old, 46%
Nose	Ginger, candied peel and apricots.
Taste	Spice, vanilla, honey and toffee.
Finish	Short and nutty.
Comments	There is more to come from this idiosyncratic distillery built on the site of a former salmon hatchery.
Also try	Talisker, Ledaig, Oban
Availability	Website and distillery only
Price	£79

Malt	Arran
Distillery	Arran
	Lochranza
	ISLE OF ARRAN
	KA27 8HJ
Owner	Isle of Arran Distillers Ltd
Visitors	Tel: 01770 830264
Website	www.arranwhisky.com
Established	1995
Status	In production
Water source	Eason Biorach
Malt source	Commercial maltsters
Phenols	Unpeated and peated to 20 ppm
Casks	Ex-bourbon barrels, ex-sherry hogsheads, butts and puncheons
Capacity	1.2 million litres of alcohol
Stills	Wash: 2 Spirit: 2
Main bottling	10 years old, 46%
Nose	Rich vanilla sweetness then exotic fruits. Complex yet harmonious.
Taste	Soft and sweet, mouth-coating with a hint of cinnamon and apple. Citrus notes against a background of sweet oak.
Finish	Long, lingering with a golden syrup feel.
Comments	Arran produces a large range of limited editions and cask-strength bottling. Now joined by its sister at Lagg which will concentrate on the peated expressions. A very popular award-winning visitor attraction.
Also try	Glenlivet, Loch Lomond, Tobermory
Availability	Widespread
Price	£38 plus

Malt	**The Hearach**
Pronounced	*heer-aach*
Distillery	Harris
	Tarbert
	ISLE OF HARRIS
	HS3 3DJ
Owner	Isle of Harris Distillers Ltd
Visitors	Tel: 01859 502212
Website	www.harrisdistillery.com
Established	2015
Status	In production
Water source	Abhainn ne Leig
Malt source	Commercial maltsters and locally sourced and malted
Phenols	12–14ppm and up to 30ppm
Casks	Ex-bourbon, ex-sherry, ex-rye and ex-Sauternes
Capacity	400,000 litres of alcohol
Stills	Wash: 1 Spirit: 1 Gin: 1
Comments	While the whisky matures try the Harris gin illustrated above. The single malt will be called The Hearach, the name given to someone from the Isle of Harris.

Malt	Highland Park
Distillery	Highland Park
	Kirkwall
	ORKNEY
	KW15 1SU
Owner	Edrington Group
Visitors	Tel: 01856 874619
Website	www.highlandparkwhisky.com
Established	1798
Status	In production
Water source	Cattie Maggie's Spring
Malt source	Floor maltings (30%) and unpeated from Simpsons
Phenols	30–40ppm from floor maltings
Casks	Refill ex-sherry Spanish and American oak and small proportion of ex-bourbon
Capacity	2.5 million litres of alcohol
Stills	Wash: 2 Spirit: 2
Main bottling	Viking Scars, 10 years old, 40%
Nose	Heather-honey sweetness with some peaty smokiness.
Taste	Rounded smoky sweetness with a full malt mouthfeel.
Finish	Teasing, heathery with subtle smoke.
Comments	Highland Park now embraces Viking branding over its extensive range.
Also try	Springbank, Scapa, Bowmore
Availability	Everywhere
Price	£45 plus

Malt	Jura
Pronounced	*JOO-ra*
Distillery	Jura
	Craighouse
	ISLE OF JURA
	PA60 7XT
Owner	Whyte & Mackay Ltd
Visitors	Tel: 01496 820385
Website	www.jurawhisky.com
Established	c.1810. Closed 1901. Rebuilt 1960–3.
Status	In production
Water source	Loch A'Bhaile Mhargaidh
Malt source	Port Ellen Maltings
Phenols	Unpeated, and up to 45ppm for Superstition
Casks	First and refill ex-bourbon, ex-sherry, French oak and ex-wine casks.
Capacity	2.4 million litres of alcohol
Stills	Wash: 2 Spirit: 2
Main bottling	10 years old, 40%
Nose	Fruit, cracked pepper and dark chocolate.
Taste	Nectarines, ginger and freshly ground coffee.
Finish	Malty with a nutty edge and some smoke.
Comments	Jura's range and maturation regime has expanded hugely. A fine island malt. The 10-year-old is matured in American white oak ex-bourbon with an Oloroso sherry cask finish.
Also try	Bowmore, Bunnahabhain, Oban
Availability	Everywhere
Price	£30 plus

Malt	Lagg
Distillery	Lagg
	Kilmory
	ISLE OF ARRAN
	KA27 8PG
Owner	Isle of Arran Distillers Ltd
Visitors	Tel: 01770 870565
Website	www.laggwhisky.com
Established	2019
Status	In production
Water source	Borehole aquifer
Malt source	Commercial maltsters
Phenols	50ppm
Casks	Mainly ex-bourbon with a variety of other types
Capacity	750,000 litres of alcohol
Stills	Wash: 1 Spirit: 1
Sample	New Make, 20cl, 63.5%
Nose	Fresh pear notes, clean and crisp with an undertone of sweet peated malt.
Taste	Light fruit and sweet notes of heather, well-balanced with a hot chilli spiciness. Undertones of rice pudding complimented with a rich campfire smoke.
Finish	Warm, mouth-coating, lively with a slight sweetness that lingers.
Comments	Lagg will eventually produce Machrie Moor, the peated expression from Isle of Arran Distillers.
Availability	At the distillery
Price	£17 for the new make.

Malt	Ledaig
Pronounced	*led-CHAIG*
Distillery	Tobermory
	ISLE OF MULL
	PA75 6NR
Owner	Burn Stewart Distillers Ltd
Visitors	Tel: 01688 302647
Website	www.ledaig.com
Established	1798
Status	In production
Water source	Gearr Abhainn
Malt source	Commercial maltsters, peated malt from Port Ellen Maltings
Phenols	38–40 ppm
Casks	Fresh and refill ex-bourbon, ex-sherry, ex-port
Capacity	1 million litres of alcohol
Stills	Wash: 2 Spirit: 2 Gin: 1
Main bottling	12 years old, 40%
Nose	Sweet briny smokiness, hints of mild antiseptic, creosote, wax polish, mint chocolate and floral seaside aromas. Soft peat, gentle smoke.
Taste	Sweet, medicinal flavours, spicy pepper, dried fruit, peat smoke, vanilla and malty creaminess.
Finish	Spicy white pepper, liquorice, cloves and a lingering saltiness.
Comments	A striking contrast to Tobermory.
Also try	Caol Ila, Talisker, Longrow
Availability	Widespread
Price	£39 plus

Malt	Raasay
Pronounce	*RAA-ssay*
Distillery	Isle of Raasay
	Borodale House
	ISLE OF RAASAY
	IV40 8PB
Owner	R&B Distillers Ltd
Visitors	Tel: 01478 470177
Website	www.raasaydistillery.com
Established	2017
Status	In production
Water source	Celtic well
Malt source	Commercial maltsters
Phenols	Peated (45ppm) and unpeated
Casks	First-fill ex-bourbon, ex-Tuscan and Bordeaux red wine, and ex-rye casks
Capacity	200,000 litres of alcohol
Stills	Wash: 1 Spirit: 1 Gin: 1
Sample	While We Wait, 2018 Release, 46%
Nose	Smokiness on first nosing, mixed with red berries, lemon and grassy notes. With more time, pear, tangerine and melon.
Taste	Dry peatiness on the palate, mixed in with red wine notes. A good dash of orange zest from the nose.
Finish	Oaky and buttery finish.
Comments	The sample is a single malt from an unnamed distillery. Raasay gin is available until the single malt is released.
Availability	Website, distillery and specialist retailers
Price	£40 plus

Malt	Scapa
Pronounced	*SKAA-pa*
Distillery	Scapa
	Kirkwall
	ORKNEY
	KW15 1SE
Owner	Pernod Ricard
Visitors	Tel: 01856 873269
Website	www.scapawhisky.com
Established	1824
Status	In production
Water source	Local springs and the Coltland Burn
Malt source	Kilgours of Kirkcaldy
Phenols	Unpeated
Casks	First-fill American oak
Capacity	1 million litres of alcohol
Stills	Wash: 1 (Lomond style) Spirit: 1
Main bottling	Skiren, NAS, 40%
Nose	Floral flavours with a hint of fresh pear. Sweet and fruity pineapple notes with a citrus tang.
Taste	Smooth and sweet, ripe honeydew melon slices, bursts of fruity pear and lemon sherbet.
Finish	Long, refreshing sweetness.
Comments	Revitalised range which includes cask-strength expressions.
Also try	Highland Park. Cragganmore, Strathisla
Availability	Specialist retailers
Price	£41 plus

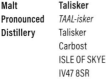

Malt	Talisker
Pronounced	*TAAL-isker*
Distillery	Talisker
	Carbost
	ISLE OF SKYE
	IV47 8SR
Owner	Diageo
Visitors	Tel: 01478 614308
Website	www.malts.com
Established	1830
Status	In production
Water source	Cnoc-nan-Speireag
Malt source	Glen Ord Maltings
Phenols	20–25 ppm
Casks	Refill American hogsheads, some refill European wood and ex-sherry
Capacity	3.3 million litres of alcohol
Stills	Wash: 2 Spirit: 3
Main bottling	10 years old, 45.8%
Nose	Powerful peat-smoke with seawater saltiness, the liquor of fresh oysters and a citrus sweetness.
Taste	Rich dried-fruit sweetness, smoke and strong barley-malt. Peppery at the back of the mouth.
Finish	Huge, long, warming and peppery in the finish with an appetising sweetness.
Comments	A consistent award-winning malt now with a much expanded range with some NAS bottlings.
Also try	Ledaig, Ardbeg, Lagavulin
Availability	Everywhere
Price	£44 plus

Mull	Tobermory
Pronounced	*tober-MORE-ay*
Distillery	Tobermory
	ISLE OF MULL
	PA75 6NR
Owner	Burn Stewart Distillers Ltd
Visitors	Tel: 01688 302647
Website	www.ledaig.com
Established	1798
Status	In production
Water source	Gearr Abhainn
Malt source	Commercial maltsters, peated malt from Port Ellen Maltings
Phenols	1–2ppm
Casks	Fresh and refill ex-bourbon, ex-sherry, ex-port
Capacity	1 million litres of alcohol
Stills	Wash: 2 Spirit: 2 Gin: 1
Main bottling	10 years old, 40%
Nose	Rich fruit, orange and citrus notes, fresh floral hints and rich oak with vanilla and spice.
Taste	Sweet orange and citrus, creamy caramel and rich vanilla with spicy hints of cinnamon and clove.
Finish	Long and lingering vanilla and spice.
Comments	Lighter than its Ledaig stablemate. The distillery is moving to gin distillation as well after some experiments during a two-year shutdown and renovation programme.
Also try	Arran, Jura, Bunnahabhain
Availability	Widespread
Price	£39 plus

Malt	Torabhaig
Pronounce	*torr-a-VAIG*
Distillery	Torabhaig
	Teangue
	ISLE OF SKYE
	IV44 8RE
Owner	Mossburn Distillers
Visitors	Tel: 01471 833447
Website	www.torabhaig.com
Established	2016
Status	In production
Water source	Allt Gleann Thorabhaig and Allt Breacach
Malt source	Crisp maltsters
Phenols	75ppm
Casks	Mostly ex-bourbon with some ex-sherry
Capacity	500,000 litres of alcohol
Stills	Wash: 1 Spirit: 1
Comments	No tasting sample available but while the maturing Torabhaig slumbers until it is ready, the distillery offers a very good visitor experience.

4. Blended Malt Scotch

BEFORE the revision of regulations in 2009 this type of Scotch whisky was known as 'vatted' malt. Why do producers bottle a mixture of malts in this fashion? In essence it is a throwback to the mid 1850s when a change in the law allowed producers to vat whiskies while still in bond. At that time the search for a more generic, palatable whisky was in full flow in order to appeal to a much wider market than the single malt (or 'self') whiskies that were then the only real option available to the drinking public. Andrew Usher then created the first vatted malt with Usher's Old Vatted Glenlivet. However, he soon realised that by combining patent-still grain whisky with a selection of malts, his aim to satisfy the desires of the public were more readily achieved and for less cost. Blended whisky became the norm and vatted malts were to remain a curiosity on the sidelines from then on.

In order to acquire a taste for single malts it could be argued that the blended malts are an intermediate step up from blended Scotch, but they are notoriously difficult to create as they lack the large canvas that is grain whisky on which the master blender is able to craft a blended Scotch from the constituent malts on his palette.

However, blended malts are widely available now on the supermarket shelves including 15-year-old Johnnie Walker Green Label and William Grant & Sons' Monkey Shoulder, which is hugely popular. Lidl's Ben Bracken brand, expertly created by Richard Paterson at Whyte & Mackay, delivers excellent value.

Given that stock management is at the core of a distiller's ability to maintain the supply of brands, it might be that more blended malts with no age statements will appear on the market as they draw from much younger stocks than they would normally do. In truth though, this category will remain small in relation to blended Scotch whisky, but it is worth venturing into nonetheless.

Brand	Abrachan
Owner	Lidl
Main bottling	Triple Wood, NAS, 42%
Nose	Rich and sherried with a sweet hint of port.
Taste	Mouth-coating, soft caramel, dried stone fruits and wild berries
Finish	Smooth and lingering.
Comments	Matured in ex-bourbon, ex-Oloroso sherry butts and ex-tawny port pipes, this is an elegant dram representing good value.
Availability	Only at Lidl
Price	£18
Website	www.lidl.co.uk

Brand	Big Peat
Owner	Douglas Laing & Co Ltd
Sample	NAS, 46%
Nose	Peaty with sweet notes of honey and toffee.
Taste	Sweet with lingering peat and a slightly floral note in the background.
Finish	Long, lingering and robust with some chocolate.
Comments	A blend of malts including Ardbeg, Caol Ila, Bowmore and Port Ellen. Also available in a number of other expressions.
Availability	Widespread
Price	£38
Website	www.douglaslaing.com

Brand	**Blooming Gorse**
Owner	Wemyss Malts
Main bottling	NAS, 46%
Nose	A fresh, bright nose with vanilla and coconut notes that weave amongst the nutty and fruity spirit to evoke the aromas of freshly bloomed gorse flowers, geraniums, honey nut cereal and roasted cashew nuts.
Taste	The initial top notes are that of rich porridge sweetened with floral honey. The mouth feel is smooth and creamy with a mild spice and tingle on the palate and the flavour of desiccated coconut.
Finish	Medium length with lingering coconut and vanilla.
Comments	One of the Wemyss Family Collection constructed with malts from two Highland distilleries.
Availability	Website and specialist retailers
Price	£46
Website	www.wemyssmalts.com

Brand	**Blue Hanger**
Owner	Berry Brothers & Rudd
Sample	11th Release, NAS, 45.6%
Nose	Orange peel, vanilla and peat smoke.
Taste	Luscious and rich fulfilling the promise of the nose.
Finish	Fruity and smoky.
Comments	William Hanger, the 3rd Lord Coleraine, was a loyal customer of BBR during the late 18th century. His wardrobe consisted largely of loud blue clothes which earned him the nickname 'Blue Hanger'.
Availability	BBR, website and specialist retailers
Price	£70
Website	www.bbr.com

Brand	Copper Dog
Owner	Craigellachie Hotel
Main bottling	NAS, 40%
Nose	Orchard fruits to the fore with sweet cereal notes.
Taste	Malty chocolate digestive biscuits with dried orange peel. Medium-bodied and mouth-coating.
Finish	Honeyed and fruity. Refreshing.
Comments	A blend of eight Speyside malts named after a utensil in which workers secreted malt whisky from the distillery.
Availability	At the hotel and specialist retailers
Price	£28

Brand	Flaming Heart
Owner	Compass Box
Main bottling	NAS, 48.9%
Nose	Ozone and salt spray, peat reek with a dash of honey and vanilla.
Taste	eat and sweet spice with dried pudding fruit.
Finish	Malty biscuits with spice. Long.
Comments	Pair this with rich cheeses after dinner.
Availability	Specialist retailers
Price	£120
Website	www.compassboxwhisky.com

Brand	Glenalmond
Owner	Vintage Malt Whisky Co
Main bottling	NAS, 40%
Nose	Sweet malt and vanilla. Caramel, spice and a touch of honey.
Taste	Soft, fruity. Gristy sugar-vanilla balance with lush sherry overtones. More spice and fruit.
Finish	Long and lingering.
Comments	Ex-bourbon and sherry matured.
Availability	Specialist retailers
Price	£28
Website	www.vintagemaltwhisky.com

Brand	Islay Journey
Owner	Hunter Laing & Co Ltd
Main bottling	NAS, 46%
Nose	Smoke, ash and tar.
Taste	Peat, sea brine, beach sand and seaweed.
Finish	Medicinal, long and intense.
Comments	A sister whisky to Highland Journey which does what it says on the label.
Availability	Specialist retailers
Price	£31
Website	www.hunterlaing.com

Brand	Johnnie Walker Green Label
Owner	Diageo
Main bottling	15 years old, 43%
Nose	Cut grass and fresh fruit mingle with pepper, rich vanilla and sandalwood.
Taste	Deep wood notes, oak and cedar. Llight garden fruits and tropical, fragrant, floral notes.
Finish	Smoky with notes of peat and sea salt.
Comments	Matured in American and European oak. Malts from Speyside, Lowlands, Highlands and Isalnds are used to create Green Label.
Availability	Widespread and specialist retailers
Price	£43
Website	www.johnniewalker.com

Brand	Monkey Shoulder
Owner	William Grant & Sons Ltd
Main bottling	NAS, 40%
Nose	Floral, citrus, peaches, apricots. Honey, oak and vanilla.
Taste	Vanilla, brown sugar, creamy toffee, oak Hints of cinnamon and nutmeg.
Finish	Smooth, lingering, sweet.
Comments	A popular and exquisitely presented blend of Glenfiddich, Balvenie and Kininvie. Ideal for cocktails.
Availability	Everywhere
Price	£27
Website	www.monkeyshoulder.com

Brand	Old Perth
Owner	Morrison & Mackay Ltd
Sample	Sherry Cask, 43%
Nose	Sweet with sherried notes.
Taste	Smooth, medium-bodied, the sherry influence to the fore.
Finish	Lingering and sweet.
Comments	Old Perth was once a well known brand name. This sherried expression was introduced in 2019.
Availability	Website and specialist retailers
Price	£30
Website	www.mandmwhisky.co.uk

Brand	Poit Dhubh
Owner	Pràban na Linne Ltd
Main bottling	12 years old, 43%
Nose	Soft smokiness, a touch of liquorice and a slight hint of citrus.
Taste	Medium-bodied, smooth with a touch of dryness. A good balance of peatiness and sweetness.
Finish	Long, smooth and smoky.
Comments	From the makers of Isle of Skye 8-year-old blended Scotch.
Availability	Website and specialist retailers
Price	£43
Website	www.gaelicwhisky.com

Brand	Rock Island
Owner	Douglas Laing & Co Ltd
Main bottling	NAS, 46.8%
Nose	Coastal shores and seaweed rocks.
Taste	Sweet peat with smoke, honey, damp ashes and a hint of black pepper.
Finish	Long, salty, peaty.
Comment	Constructed from a mélange of Islay, Arran, Orkney and Jura malts. Once known as Rock Oyster.
Availability	Website and specialist retailers
Price	£38
Website	www.douglaslaing.com

Brand	Shackleton
Owner	Whyte & Mackay Ltd
Main bottling	NAS, 40%
Nose	Vanilla, toffee apple, cinnamon and ginger.
Taste	Dark sugar, sweet dried fruits and glazed pineapple.
Finish	Hot mulled wine, praline chocolate and a wisp of bonfire smoke.
Comments	Created from bottles discovered under the Nimrod expedition hut in Antarctica that had remained undisturbed since 1907.
Availability	Widespread and specialist retailers
Price	£35
Website	www.theshackletonwhisky.com

Brand	Sheep Dip
Owner	Ian Macleod Distillers Ltd
Main bottling	NAS, 40%
Nose	Beach air, malty, honey and caramel.
Taste	Full, malty, zesty, rich.
Finish	That tanginess lingers.
Comments	A brand with an interesting back story now under new ownership. Well worth searching out. Sixteen malts go into this dram, aged between 8 and 21 years so there's a bit of quality here.
Availability	Website and specialist retailers
Price	£29
Website	www.ianmacleod.com

Brand	Spice Tree
Owner	Compass Box
Main bottling	NAS, 46%
Nose	Cloves, ginger, cinnamon, nutmeg and vanilla.
Taste	Full, round and sweet with spice and vanilla.
Finish	Long and lingering.
Comments	A blend of aged Northern Highland malts. Matured in American oak then custom-made barrels using heavily toasted new French oak heads from the Vosges forest.
Availability	Website and specialist retailers
Price	£45
Website	www.compassboxwhisky.com

Brand	Timorous Beastie
Owner	Douglas Laing & Co Ltd
Main bottling	NAS, 46.8%
Nose	Sweet initially, then warming to floral, light barley and spicy honeyed tones.
Taste	Spicy with fruit notes of raisin and sugary vanilla.
Finish	Subtle yet sweet with real oaky flavour, hints of milky cereals and late meringue.
Comments	The constituent Highland malts are Dalmore, Glengoyne, Blair Athol and Glen Garioch.
Availability	Website and specialist retailers
Price	£38
Website	www.douglaslaing.com

Brand	Vanilla Burst
Owner	Wemyss Malts
Main bottling	NAS, 46%
Nose	Peaches, lemon toffee bonbons and pineapple syrup with creamy vanilla and buttery shortbread.
Taste	Tingling spice and zesty orange peel, freshly grated ginger and honey.
Finish	Toffee and hazelnut with hints of spicy oak and lingering vanilla.
Comments	Two Speyside malts matured in first-fill ex-bourbon make up this blended malt with a heavy vanilla influence.
Availability	Website and specialist retailers
Price	£44
Website	www.wemyssmalts.com

5. Single Grain Scotch

VERY few proprietary brand single grain whiskies are on the market. Diageo's Cameron Brig has been there longest and was joined a couple of years ago by Haig Club and then Haig Clubman has been backed by David Beckham. Loch Lomond also sells a single grain, as do Arbikie and BrewDog is working on its version as rye makes its return to the Scotch portfolio. The other bottlings come from the independents who have secured stocks from Scotland's grain distillers, past and present. One distillery not included in this section is Starlaw near Cumbernauld which is distilling exclusively for La Martiniquaise brands, such as Glen Turner, almost all of it for the French market.

It is not surprising that single grain whisky is not well known. It has always been considered the sleeping partner in the make-up of a Scotch blend, but this ignores the fact that grain spirit must have 'an aroma and taste derived from the raw materials used in, and the method of, its production.' That requirement is legal in order for it to be termed Scotch grain whisky. It might be high in strength, but neutral and flavourless it can never be.

Grain whiskies also vary in the way they are produced as some distillers employ the basic two-column set up (see 5) producing a fairly full and oily distillate whereas others have multiple columns giving a cleaner and lighter spirit. The result is that Scotland's seven grain distilleries produce differing grain whiskies with distinct distillery character.

First-fill ex-bourbon casks are preferred for grain whisky maturation and give vanilla and coconut notes as well as mellowing the spirit which can be metallic when new. Over time it is sweetened until, when fully mature, it coats the mouth with a luxurious vanilla character. Most grains take well to being much longer in cask than malt and some of the vintage independent bottlings can stand up to many single malts. They may be few in number, but they are worth the effort to track down and try, although your pockets might have to be deep.

Grain	**Cameron Brig**
Distillery	Cameron Bridge WINDYGATES KY8 5RL
Owner	Diageo
Established	1824
Status	In production
Water source	Borehole aquifers
Cereals source	Wheat from East Coast of Scotland, malt from Burghead Maltings
Phenols	Unpeated
Casks	First fill and refill ex-bourbon
Capacity	100 million litres of alcohol
Main bottling	NAS, 40%
Nose	Slight, with some spice, vanilla and a hint of oak.
Taste	Some dried fruit, citrus with a hint of sherry-oak and caramel.
Finish	Smooth and mouth-coating with oak nuances.
Comments	Also available as Haig Club and Clubman.
Availability	Specialist retailers
Price	£23 plus

Grain	Girvan
Distillery	Girvan
	GIRVAN
	KA26 9PY
Owner	William Grant & Sons Ltd
Established	1964
Status	In production
Water source	Penwhapple Reservoir
Cereals source	Commercial grain dealers
Phenols	Unpeated
Casks	Ex-bourbon
Capacity	115 million litres of alcohol
Main bottling	Patent Still, No 4 Apps, NAS, 42%
Nose	Vanilla, green apple skins.
Taste	Citrus and sugar, vanilla and oak with a hint of honey.
Finish	Quick and sweet with a trace of pepper.
Comments	Apps stands for the distilling Apparatus.
Availability	Specialist retailers
Price	£45 plus

Grain	Invergordon
Distillery	Invergordon
	INVERGORDON
	IV18 0HP
Owner	Whyte & Mackay Ltd
Established	1961
Status	In production
Water source	Loch Glass
Cereals source	Wheat and barley from the east of Scotland
Casks	Ex-bourbon
Capacity	36 million litres of alcohol
Sample	10 years old, 55.4%
Nose	Vanilla, menthol, spice.
Taste	Notes of almond biscuits with a toasted edge.
Finish	Coconut and vanilla.
Comments	From That Boutique-y Whisky Company; other bottlings are available but can be expensive.
Availability	Independent bottlers and specialist retailers
Price	£38 plus

Grain	Loch Lomond
Distillery	Loch Lomond
	ALEXANDRIA
	G83 0TL
Owner	Loch Lomond Group
Website	www.lochlomondwhiskies.com
Established	1966
Status	In production
Water source	Borehole aquifers and Loch Lomond
Cereals source	Commercial grain dealers
Phenols	Unpeated
Casks	Ex-bourbon
Capacity	20 million litres of alcohol
Main bottling	NAS, 46%
Nose	Soft and sweet.
Taste	Light, sweet and buttery with vanilla tones.
Finish	Refreshing and clean.
Comments	Made from 100& malted barley, but cannot be called malt whisky.
Availability	Website and specialist retailers
Price	£27 plus

Grain	North British
Distillery	North British
	EDINBURGH
	EH11 2PX
Owner	Lothian Distillers Ltd
Website	www.northbritish.co.uk
Established	1887
Status	In production
Water source	Pentland Hills reservoirs
Cereals source	Maltings on site with 25% of cereal mash as malted barley, the remainder is maize
Phenols	Unpeated
Casks	Ex-bourbon
Capacity	73 million litres of alcohol
Sample	Signatory, 10 years old, 43%
Nose	Melon and vanilla.
Taste	Citrus and cereal grains with a hint of spice.
Finish	Quick, brisk, a hint of mint.
Comments	The distillery is jointly owned by Diageo and the Edrington Group.
Availability	Independent bottlers and specialist retailers
Price	£25 plus

Grain	**Strathclyde**
Distillery	Strathclyde
	Moffat Street
	GLASGOW
	G5 0QB
Owner	Pernod Ricard
Established	1927
Status	In production
Water source	Mains water from Loch Katrine
Cereals source	Local commercial maltsters and grain suppliers.
Phenols	Unpeated
Casks	Ex-bourbon
Capacity	40 million litres of alcohol
Sample	Claxton's, 26 years old, 50.6%
Nose	Caramel and banana with vanilla.
Taste	Vanilla and shortbread.
Finish	Banana, caramel and vanilla.
Comments	Strathclyde was once home to Kinclaith Distillery (see 99).
Availability	Very rare. Independent bottlers and specialist retailers
Price	£100 plus

6. Blended Grain Scotch

WHILE the blended malt category has grown over the past decade, the same cannot be said of blended grain whisky. Of the big players only the Edrington Group has ventured here with The Snow Grouse, a whisky that was designed to be served chilled, but it has since been discontinued. Unlike a chilled vodka, this type of Scotch has been influenced by the wood in which the constituent grains have matured, so the experience is more rewarding. Compass Box has continued to release Hedonism which is a complex blend of three single grain whiskies. Similarly North Star Spirits has released a 36-year-old blended grain.

This category would probably not exist had it not been for Compass Box's founder, John Glaser, who recognised that the single grain whiskies produced in Scotland were worth exploring, blending and then bottling. But blended grain is still a very rare beast and it is unlikely to expand much over the coming years. It is more likely that single grain whiskies will continue to grow as increasingly informed drinkers appreciate what they have to offer.

Brand	Hedonism
Owner	Compass Box
Main bottling	NAS, 43%
Nose	Elegant with vanilla to the fore.
Taste	Vanilla, pastry cream, toffee and coconut.
Finish	Silky, creamy oak.
Comments	Sourced from Cameron Bridge, Carsebridge and Cambus, Port Dundas or Dumbarton, aged between 14 and 25 years and matured in first-fill American oak barrels and rejuvenated American oak hogsheads.
Availability	Website and specialist retailers
Price	£58
Website	www.compassboxwhisky.com

Brand	North Star
Owner	North Star Spirits
Main bottling	36 years old, 52.5%
Nose	Charred oak and poached plums.
Taste	Hard toffee, French freshly baked patisserie.
Finish	Dry, long and salty.
Comments	An outturn of 288 bottles from unnamed grain distilleries.
Availability	Website and specialist retailers
Price	£146 plus
Website	www.northstarspirits.com

7. Blended Scotch

TO cover all the available Scotch blends would mean writing another couple of books on this category alone. The ones I am listing here are a representative selection of some of the blends to be found in supermarkets and High Street wine and spirit merchants, global travel retail (GTR), specialist retailers and from independent bottlers.

You will come across many Scotch blends, especially when airside or in GTR which will be unfamiliar to you. The reason is that distillers have built up some brands exclusively in export markets and have UK brands for the home market as well. One such brand from Bacardi, William Lawson, is ubiquitous in Europe but is uncommon in the UK. The range of selected blended whiskies in this section covers a selection from the higher priced premium (also known as deluxe) category, right down to the sorts of whiskies you will encounter on the gantry in your local pub.

Blends are commonly categorised by price with NAS bottlings available between £10 and £20, and the premium, age-statement blends like Chivas Regal coming in above the £20 mark. These blends contain a higher proportion of malts than the NAS blends (although the non-premium Teacher's Highland Cream is the exception to this rule with a malt content of 45%). It goes without saying that the grain whiskies used in a premium blend are also aged and of a very high quality.

Although the expectation of most newcomers to Scotch whisky might be that a lot of blends are likely to be quite similar, the art of the master blender assures that there is plenty of variety in style and character from light and creamy to full-bodied and smoky over a wide price range. In short, blended Scotch whiskies offer something for everyone – which is exactly what Andrew Usher envisaged when he created the first blended Scotch over 150 years ago.

Brand	**The Antiquary**
Owner	Takara Shuzo Company
Main bottling	NAS, 40%
Nose	Clean and soft with vanilla, orange, lemon and very light smoke.
Taste	Fresh. A balance of mellow grain with ripe fruity malt. Some heathery notes coming through.
Finish	Medium. Soft with a light smokiness.
Comments	A famous Victorian brand named after one of Sir Walter Scott's characters.
Availability	Specialist retailers
Price	£18
Website	www.theantiquary.com

Brand	**Ballantine's**
Owner	Pernod Ricard
Main bottling	Finest, NAS, 40%
Nose	Heather honey with a hint of spice.
Taste	Fresh. A balance of milk chocolate, red apple and vanilla.
Finish	Fresh and floral.
Comments	Still made to the original 1910 recipe. A classic blended Scotch.
Availability	Website and specialist retailers
Price	£19
Website	www.ballantines.com

Brand	Bank Note
Owner	AD Rattray
Main bottling	5 years old, 43%
Nose	Clean, crisp aroma, hints of vanilla.
Taste	Mellow on the taste with sweet richness and depth of flavour.
Finish	Clean on the palate with lingering sweetness.
Comments	A relaunched brand with a healthy 40% malt content.
Availability	Website and specialist retailers
Price	£21
Website	www.adrattray.com

Brand	Bell's
Owner	Diageo
Main bottling	Original, NAS, 40%
Nose	Soft, gentle with hints of barley. Quite floral.
Taste	Fresh. Smooth, medium-bodied with cereal, oak and spice overtones.
Finish	Quite short but pleasant with a trace of smoke and some fruitcake.
Comments	Britain's most popular blend of Scotch.
Availability	Everywhere
Price	£16

Brand	**Black Bottle**
Owner	Burn Stewart Distillers Ltd
Main bottling	NAS, 40%
Nose	Fresh and floral with freshly-sawn oak aromas. Spicy with hints of smoke.
Taste	Silky, mellow and fruity with balanced smoky-peaty flavours, then sweet oak and heather honey.
Finish	Soft, spicy, nutmeg, pepper and lingering smokiness.
Comments	Relaunched in 2013 and double-matured in charred virgin oak.
Availability	Widespread and specialist retailers
Price	£19
Website	www.blackbottle.com

Brand	**Chivas Regal**
Owner	Pernod Ricard
Main bottling	12 years old, 40%
Nose	Wild herbs, heather honey and orchard fruits.
Taste	Full and round with honey, ripe pears, vanilla, hazelnut and butterscotch.
Finish	Lingering and rich.
Comments	A classic premium blend.
Availability	Everywhere
Price	£26
Website	www.chivas.com

Brand	Cutty Sark
Owner	Edrington Group
Main bottling	NAS, 40%
Nose	Fresh and citrusy.
Taste	Vanilla and citrus fruits.
Finish	Zesty, vanilla ice cream with notes of caramel.
Comments	Purchased from BBR in 2010, this brand now has an expanded range.
Availability	Widespread and specialist retailers
Price	£20
Website	www.cutty-sark.com

Brand	Dewar's
Owner	John Dewar & Sons Ltd
Main bottling	White Label, NAS, 40%
Nose	Honey, citrus fruits.
Taste	Pears with hints of smoke, heather honey and oak.
Finish	The sweet honey lingers.
Comments	Over 40 malts go into this historic blend with Aberfeldy at its heart.
Availability	Widespread and specialist retailers
Price	£20
Website	www.dewars.com

Brand	Famous Grouse
Owner	Edrington Group
Main bottling	NAS, 40%
Nose	Candied fruits, buttery shortbread, citrus peel.
Taste	Dried fruit, cinnamon and ginger, hint of oak.
Finish	Smooth, well balanced.
Comments	Scotland's favourite blended Scotch.
Availability	Everywhere
Price	£10
Website	www.thefamousgrouse.com

Brand	Grant's
Owner	William Grant & Sons Ltd
Main bottling	Family Reserve, NAS, 40%
Nose	Clean with hints of banana.
Taste	Complex banana and vanilla sweetness balancing sharper malty tones.
Finish	Medium length and sweet.
Comments	An award-winning blend from the owners of Glenfiddich.
Availability	Widespread and specialist retailers
Price	£17
Website	www.grantswhisky.com

Brand	**Great King Street**
Owner	Compass Box
Main bottling	Artist's Blend, NAS, 43%
Nose	Full and rich.
Taste	Round and fruity with hints of toasty oak, vanilla and spice.
Finish	Well balanced and lengthy.
Comments	A masterful marriage of malt and grain. Also available as the Glasgow Blend.
Availability	Website and specialist retailers
Price	£36
Website	www.compassboxwhisky.com

Brand	**Hankey Bannister**
Owner	Burn Stewart Distillers Ltd
Main bottling	Original, NAS, 40%
Nose	Light and spicy.
Taste	Light and clean, sweet, spicy with honeyed tones.
Finish	Long-lasting with a touch of sweet fudge.
Comments	A famous brand which is an ideal cocktail whisky.
Availability	Specialist retailers
Price	£20
Website	www.hankeybannister.com

Brand	High Commissioner
Owner	Loch Lomond Group
Main bottling	NAS, 40%
Nose	Fruity and light, pears and peaches.
Taste	Sweet and fruity with notes of malted barley, overlaid with a touch of peat and chewy caramel.
Finish	Long-lasting and warm.
Comments	One of the top selling blends in the UK.
Availability	Everywhere
Price	£15
Website	www.lochlomondgroup.com

Brand	Isle of Skye
Owner	Ian Macleod Distillers Ltd
Main bottling	8 years old, 40%
Nose	Peat, oak and vanilla.
Taste	Sweet and mouth-coating, barley sugar, spice and peat.
Finish	Sweet, spicy and oaky.
Comments	An evocative name and an excellent blend to sip and savour.
Availability	Widespread, website and specialist retailers
Price	£20
Website	www.isleofskyewhisky.com

Brand	J&B
Owner	Diageo
Main bottling	NAS, 40%
Nose	Citrus zest and malt.
Taste	Fruity and well-rounded with hints of toffee.
Finish	Oak and spice.
Comments	Found on gantries around the world.
Availability	Everywhere
Price	£19
Website	www.jbscotch.com

Brand	Johnnie Walker Black Label
Owner	Diageo
Main bottling	12 years old, 40%
Nose	Rich, dark fruit and a hint of sweet vanilla.
Taste	Vanilla to the fore, orange zest and aromas of spice and raisins.
Finish	Rich smoke, peat, and malt.
Comments	Twenty-nine distilleries contribute to the world's bestselling premium blend.
Availability	Everywhere
Price	£27
Website	www.johnniewalker.com

Brand	Johnnie Walker Red Label
Owner	Diageo
Main bottling	NAS, 40%
Nose	Fresh, fruity, spicy and smoky.
Taste	Spicy with cinnamon and fresh black pepper.
Finish	Long and smoky.
Comments	The world's bestselling Scotch blend.
Availability	Everywhere
Price	£21
Website	www.johnniewalker.com

Brand	Lismore
Owner	J&G Grant
Main bottling	Special Reserve, 8 years old, 40%
Nose	Cinnamon spice and caramel with toasted malt.
Taste	Cinnamon again, brown sugar. Hints of sherry.
Finish	Vanilla and sharp peppery spice.
Comments	Not well known, but worth a try. Good value too.
Availability	Specialist retailers
Price	£21

Brand	Loch Lomond
Owner	Loch Lomond Group
Sample	Signature, NAS, 40%
Nose	Sherried notes and dark fruits.
Taste	Soft and creamy with soft fruits and vanilla and a hint of rich dried cake fruits.
Finish	Peach and apricot fading to dried fruits.
Comments	Loch Lomond uses a solera system where whiskies are married in a 100-cask blending vat prior to bottling. This brand has been rejuvenated since the Bulloch family sold it in 2014 and it is now under new ownership again.
Availability	Website and specialist retailers
Price	£26
Website	www.lochlomondwhiskies.com

Brand	Mackinlay's
Owner	Whyte & Mackay Ltd
Sample	Original, NAS, 40%
Nose	Spicy and smoky.
Taste	Vanilla and ginger with hints of honey.
Finish	Slightly smoky and honeyed.
Comments	A famous brand that was closely associated with Sir Ernest Shackleton's expeditions to the Antarctic.
Availability	Widespread and specialist retailers
Price	£32

Brand	Nevis Dew
Owner	Asahi Group Holdings
Main bottling	Special Reserve, NAS, 40%
Nose	Malty with smoke, some peat, honey and spice.
Taste	Oak and toffee, some peat with sweet tablet.
Finish	Oak, fudge and peat.
Comments	Not widely available but good value and worth trying.
Availability	Specialist retailers
Price	£20

Brand	Outlaw King
Owner	Annandale Distillery Co Ltd
Main bottling	NAS, 40%
Nose	Green apple, honey, toffee and vanilla.
Taste	Smoke, pineapple, nectarine and mango.
Finish	Long, with orange peel, pine resin and peat smoke.
Comments	Inspired by the story of King Robert the Bruce, 7th Lord of Annandale, who defeated the English at Bannockburn in 1314.
Availability	Website and specialist retailers
Price	£31
Website	www.annandaledistillery.com

Brand	Pure Scot
Owner	Bladnoch Distillery Ltd
Main bottling	NAS, 40%
Nose	Rich and fragrant. Old leather, toffee and fruitcake, malty with a hint of smoke.
Taste	Full-bodied and mellow. Rich smokiness with ginger marmalade, sweet honeyed fruit and slightly peppery.
Finish	Spicy and smoky, long-lasting.
Comments	Aged Bladnoch malt mixed with malts from Islay, the Highlands and Speyside and other malt and grain whiskies.
Availability	Website and specialist retailers
Price	£40 plus
Website	www.purescot.com

Brand	Robert Burns
Owner	Isle of Arran Distillers Ltd
Main bottling	NAS, 40%
Nose	Raspberry and almond tart with hints of toasted oak and toffee.
Taste	Dry, light with hints of sweet apple and liquorice. A hint of peat smoke appears in the background.
Finish	Fresh, warming with lingering vanilla sweetness.
Comments	The only whisky approved by the Robert Burns World Federation.
Availability	Website and specialist retailers
Price	£20
Website	www.robertburnswhisky.com

Brand	Teacher's Highland Cream
Owner	Beam Suntory
Main bottling	NAS, 40%
Nose	Malty, with pronounced but gentle peat followed by orchard fruits and honey.
Taste	Full and rich. Slowly fades to a silky roundness.
Finish	Well balanced with a clean, busy fullness that lingers.
Comments	One of the highest malt contents of any NAS blend with 45%.
Availability	Widespread and specialist retailers
Price	£18
Website	www.teacherswhisky.com

Brand	Whyte & Mackay
Owner	Whyte & Mackay Ltd
Main bottling	Special, NAS, 40%
Nose	Marzipan, Manuka honey, caramel Demerara sugar, hints of glazed pineapple, cider apples and praline chocolate.
Taste	Tropical fruits, rosehip syrup, caramelised orange and macaroons.
Finish	Peaches in syrup, liquorice and Seville marmalade.
Comments	Very popular in the West of Scotland and beautifully presented.
Availability	Everywhere
Price	£17
Website	www.whyteandmackay.com

8. Lost malt and grain distilleries since 1960

WHISKY from these distilleries is available at auction and from specialist retailers. Prices vary but tend to be high and an ever-dwindling supply means those prices will only rise. You won't find any Parkmore as it reputedly produced poor whisky and only operated for 37 years. Malt Mill, which was incorporated into the Lagavulin site, is also unobtainable.

SPEYSIDE
Caperdonich 1898–2010
Coleburn 1897–1985 (mothballed)
Convalmore 1894–1985
   (mothballed)
Dallas Dhu 1899–1983
   (mothballed)
Imperial 1897–2014
Parkmore 1894–1931
   (mothballed)
Pittyvaich 1974–93

EASTERN HIGHLANDS
Banff 1863–1983
Glenesk/Hillside 1897–1985
Glenugie c.1831–1968
Glenury Royal c.1825–1985
Lochside 1957–96 (also distilled
   grain whisky)
North Port/Brechin c.1820–1983

NORTHERN HIGHLANDS
Ben Wyvis 1965–77
Brora 1819–1983 (now being
   reinstated by Diageo)
Glen Albyn c.1846–1983
Glen Mhor 1892–1983
Millburn c.1807–1985

WESTERN HIGHLANDS
Glenlochy 1898–1983
Loch Ewe 2006–17

LOWLANDS
Inverleven 1938–91
Kinclaith 1956/7–76/7
Ladyburn 1966–75
Littlemill 1772–1984
Moffat (Glen Flagler/Killyloch)
   1965–86
St Magdalene c.1798–1983

Grain Distilleries
Caledonian (1855–1988)
Cambus (1806–1993)
Carsebridge (1799–1983)
Garnheath (1965–86)
Port Dundas (1810–2010)

ISLAY
Malt Mill 1908–62
Port Ellen 1825–1983 (now being
   reinstated by Diageo)

CAMPBELTOWN
Seventeen distilleries closed in
the 1920s, but none since and
Glengyle was reinstated in 2004.

Index of brands and distilleries